HOW TO FLY
A PLANE

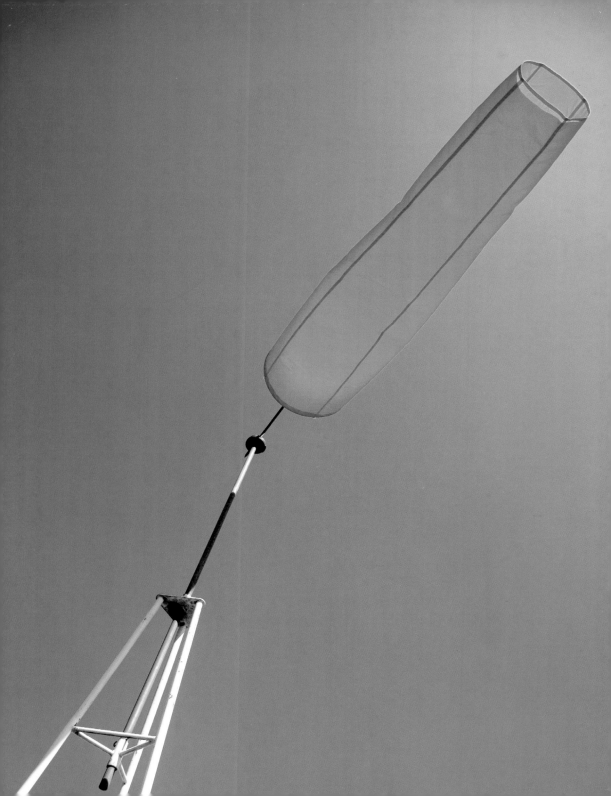

HOW TO FLY A PLANE

NICK BARNARD

PHOTOGRAPHY BY LUCY POPE

WITH 209 COLOR ILLUSTRATIONS

ABRAMS IMAGE
NEW YORK

For my mother, who helped me rediscover my father's love for flying

This book is not intended as an instruction manual and should not be treated as such. Learning to fly requires professional instruction at a properly accredited flight school.

First published in the United States of America in 2008 by
Abrams Image
An imprint of Harry N. Abrams, Inc.

First published in the United Kingdom in 2007 by
Thames & Hudson Ltd, London

How to Fly a Plane © 2007 Thames & Hudson Ltd, London
Text © Nick Barnard
Photographs © 2007 Lucy Pope

Cataloging-in-Publication data has been applied for and may be obtained from the Library of Congress.

ISBN 978-0-8109-9544-4

Designed by Thames & Hudson

Printed and bound in China by Everbest Printing Co. Ltd
10 9 8 7 6 5 4 3 2 1

HNA ■■■■■■
harry n. abrams, inc.
a subsidiary of La Martinière Groupe

115 West 18th Street
New York, NY 10011
www.hnabooks.com

Contents

Introduction

There's something extraordinary about flying a plane – or even flying in a plane. As the wheels cease rolling on the ground, and the wings lift you skywards, you're released from the earth and move freely in a new dimension where your world is the air outside, with just the flying machine around you. This is a powerful sensation and a truly profound experience, particularly when you are flying on your own as you, and you alone, are wholly responsible for your actions. You will need all your skills, training, experience and judgment to master the aircraft and the conditions in which you find yourself. It's a compelling challenge that requires planning, accuracy, sensitivity and focus, but the reward is exquisite: the freedom of the sky.

The unique thrill of flying a plane is the essence of, and the inspiration for, this book. This is not a theory or course-related handbook, and should not be treated as such; it's a practical guide on how to start flying and a celebration of the many exciting possibilities for flight in our age. The book is divided into three chapters which cover all the basics, as well as giving a taster of what it's like to fly a plane for the very first time. Within the reference pages, 'Pilot's Notes', is an invaluable selection of useful links and contacts so that you can take the next step to finding the right organization, manufacturer, supplier or training school for your needs.

'How a Plane Flies', the very first chapter, is an easy-to-use, illustrated guide to aerodynamics and engines, with a particular focus on the forces at work on a plane: lift (the upward force that keeps a plane in the air), thrust (the force that moves a plane forward), drag (air resistance holding a plane back) and weight (pulling a plane down). Novice pilots will find this chapter particularly useful, as it takes complicated concepts and breaks them down into an accessible format.

'Let's Go Flying' leads you through the various stages of flying a plane, step by step, by putting you in the pilot's seat. Using the latest training plane, a Diamond Star DA40 TDI, you will be able to follow all the stages of a training flight from a pilot's perspective, from the moment you start up the engine to the end of the flight.

The third chapter, 'First Flights', offers a unique opportunity to experience what it's like to fly eight different planes for the very first time. From a high-performance glider to the luxurious Learjet, you will be taken on a tour of each aircraft, its features and design details. The excitement of flight will be revealed in all its forms – from slow to fast planes, from historic biplanes of wood and fabric to stunt machines made of exotic composites, and from a four-seater training aircraft to a passenger jet.

Flying a plane has always been exciting, demanding and rewarding, whether it be in vintage biplanes on historic and heroic escapades or when testing the latest extreme aerospace designs and control systems. Since the early days of flying, as our understanding of flight and technology has grown, planes have naturally evolved and developed accordingly. What makes our age so different, so full of opportunity, is the imaginative combining of tradition, technology and passion that is so apparent today and has created a new world of choice for pilots.

Flying has never been so enticing. New types of easy-to-fly, low-cost planes make learning cheaper (in relative terms, of course) than ever before. The latest designs in touring aircraft are more efficient, faster, quieter and safer, and the handling – the feel of the plane – has improved as well. Accurate and easy-to-use navigation equipment is inexpensive and, when used correctly, offers a real improvement in flight safety. At a glance you are able to pinpoint your precise location and destination, better equipping you to cover all the essentials in your own aircraft and keep an eye out for other aviators. In this exciting age in aviation, vintage, historic and classic plane designs are increasingly being restored and maintained for private and public use. Want to fly a Tiger Moth, Mustang, Hawker Hunter, MiG interceptor or Dakota? There are operators out there ready to offer you the flight of a lifetime.

Have fun and fly safely.

1 How a Plane Flies

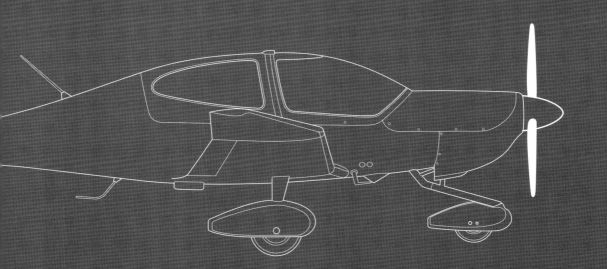

The Structure of a Plane

By aerodynamic necessity most planes essentially look very similar and are made up of a body, or fuselage, supporting a payload, passengers or cargo, to which the wings and a tail are attached. Unless you're flying a glider, there'll be an engine or engines attached to the structure to provide thrust. The illustrations of the Diamond Star DA40 TDI, opposite and overleaf, highlight some of the generic interior and exterior features.

Fuselage: The Body

The fuselage is the central structure of the plane, carrying one or more pilots and a payload. Attached to the fuselage are the wings and the tail. Single-engine planes are usually powered by an engine fitted within, or onto, the fuselage.

Wings: The Lifting Force

The wings are the main lifting surface of a plane, which takes flight when sufficient airflow over the wings creates an upward force that supports the craft in flight. The wings often hold fuel in suitably shaped tanks. Engines powering multi-engine planes are usually attached to the wings.

Tail: The Stabilizing Force

The tail is made up of a fin or vertical stabilizer, and a tailplane or horizontal stabilizer, which provide balance.

Cockpit: The Control Centre

Most planes are designed with a side-by-side cockpit (i.e. with space for two people to sit alongside). The pilot in command, or captain, sits on the left-hand side as you face forward. Some two-seater training planes have a tandem cockpit in which the pupil and instructor sit one in front of the other. This makes for a slender and aerodynamically efficient fuselage, but at the expense of a seating arrangement that allows you to monitor directly the actions of your fellow pilot.

Primary Control Surfaces

The attitude (the position in flight) of the plane is adjusted by moving the control surfaces (the elevator and the rudder in the tail, and the ailerons on the wings) using the control column and rudder pedals within the cockpit. These control surfaces therefore also determine the direction in which the plane flies.

The elevator controls the pitching movement (nose up or down) and is deflected by moving the control column backwards or forwards. The control column itself, which is located in the cockpit, is usually one of three types: a floor-mounted stick, a control wheel or yoke that can be floor-mounted or located in the instrument panel, or a side stick.

Each wing has an aileron; these control rolling movements and deflect when you move the control column from side to side. The rudder controls the yawing motion of the nose from side to side and is deflected by pushing on the rudder pedals with your feet.

Undercarriage or Landing Gear

The undercarriage is the wheeled structure underneath an aircraft which supports it on the ground. Planes have either a fixed or retractable undercarriage. This is made up of the main gear – the load-bearing main wheels, brakes and oleos – as well as either a nose wheel (as in the case of tricycle planes) or a tail wheel (for taildragger planes), which is often used for steering and is usually operated with the rudder pedals.

Engine: Pull or Push?

Most light aircraft are powered by piston petrol engines which are cooled by the flow of air passing over the engine. These are known as air-cooled engines. The engine's power is converted to thrust by a propeller. Some propeller-driven planes have piston diesel engines (light aircraft); others have a version of a jet engine commonly known as a turboprop. Pure jet engines create thrust by sucking in air and blowing it out at high speed, using the energy from the combustion of jet fuel.

Cockpit Controls in a Diamond Star DA40 TDI

1 Throttle
2 Control column
3 Rudder
4 Parking brake
5 Flap switch
6 Master switch and start
7 Standby altimeter, airspeed indicator and altitude indicator and compass
8 Navigation and engine instruments screen and radio controls
9 Flight instruments screen and radio controls
10 Transponder
11 Avionics switch
12 Light switches
13 Engine test switches
14 Circuit breakers
15 Pitot heat switch

Anatomy of a Diamond Star DA40 TDI

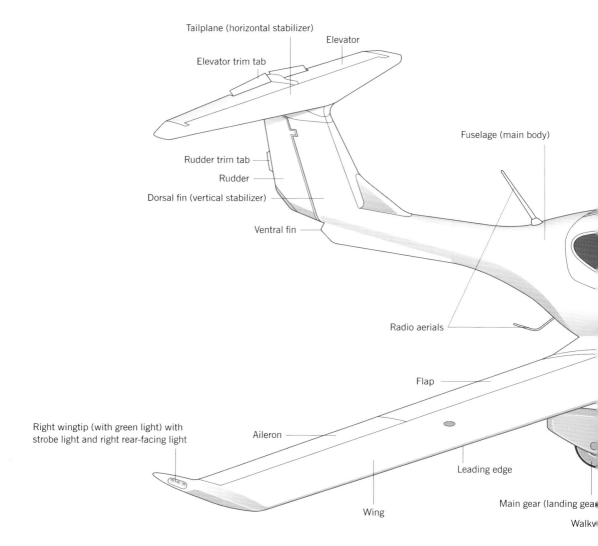

Tailplane (horizontal stabilizer)

Elevator

Elevator trim tab

Fuselage (main body)

Rudder trim tab

Rudder

Dorsal fin (vertical stabilizer)

Ventral fin

Radio aerials

Flap

Right wingtip (with green light) with
strobe light and right rear-facing light

Aileron

Leading edge

Wing

Main gear (landing gea

Walkv

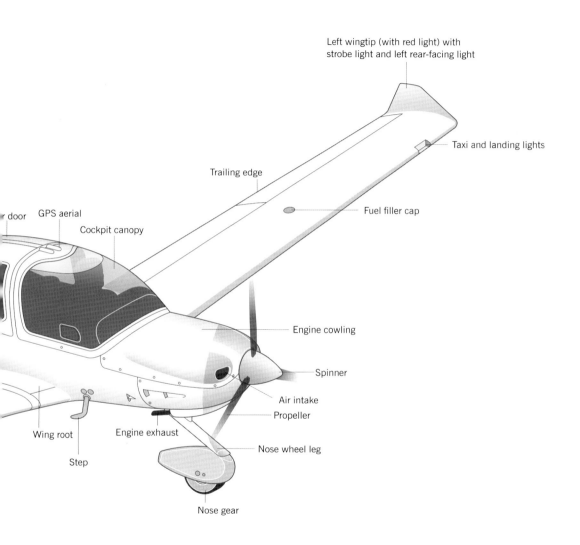

Left wingtip (with red light) with strobe light and left rear-facing light

Taxi and landing lights

Trailing edge

door

GPS aerial

Cockpit canopy

Fuel filler cap

Engine cowling

Spinner

Air intake

Propeller

Wing root

Engine exhaust

Nose wheel leg

Step

Nose gear

Balancing Weight with Lift, and Drag with Thrust

Whether you're flying in an Airbus or a glider, the forces that act on a plane are identical. In straight and level steady flight, lift balances weight, and thrust balances drag [1].

Lift and Weight

A plane's weight, acting downwards, is balanced by the lift force, acting upwards, generated by a flow of air over the wings. Look at the Airbus A380: its wings, with a span of almost 80 m (262 ft), generate enough lift to support a plane that can weigh over 500,000 kg (1,100,000 lb). How? Well, as indicated, it's all about the way in which air flows past a shaped object, but particularly how this is affected by the angle at which the two meet. When air passes over the wing of a plane in a smooth flow, it is deflected downwards (known as downwash), and the pressure on the underside of the wing caused by this deflection of air creates an opposite force, up. Did you ever as a child idle away your time by sticking your hand out of the window of a moving car on a warm summer's day? If you did, you would have discovered that your hand stayed level if you kept it horizontal (parallel to the airflow), but the moment you raised it at an angle, even slightly, it felt like it wanted to fly upwards and backwards. And, of course, if you allowed your hand to drop at an angle below the horizontal, it was forced down and back. Your hand was acting as a crude aerofoil, or wing. And the angle at which a wing meets the airflow is known as the angle of attack.

It sounds simple and it is. But it is worth noting that the angle of attack describes the angle at which the wing meets the airflow, and this has nothing to do with the direction in which the plane is pointing against the horizon, which is known as the attitude. Imagine a plane in a vertical climb, using its excess speed to gain height; here, despite the high-nose attitude, the air meets the wing at a shallow angle. This is described more fully on pages 16–17.

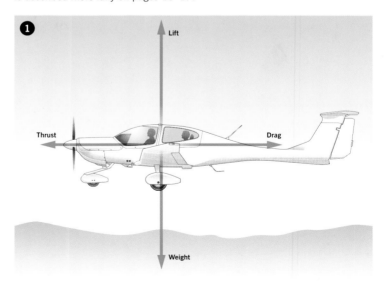

1

Lift

Thrust

Drag

Weight

So, as the air passes over the wing in a smooth flow, the flow is directed downwards. In essence the wing is pushing the air down. Another way of understanding this force is to visualize a plane, in straight and level flight, passing through a cloud of thick smoke [2]. As the plane passes through the smoke cloud in level flight, its wings push the smoke down. In pushing down, an opposite force is created upwards [3]. This is the lifting force that keeps the plane aloft.

This downward force against the air is considerable. We tend to think of air as light, but at sea level air is actually rather heavy, weighing in at about 1.29 kg (2.84 lb) per cubic metre at 20°C (68°F). In contrast, air becomes thinner and lighter as you ascend or as it is heated, which is why a typical wing is more effective at creating lift at sea level, where the air is thicker and cooler.

Drag and Thrust

Most planes that can travel at high speeds, such as supersonic fighters, look sleek and arrowlike, whereas an old training biplane may well look beautiful in a classic sort of way, but not streamlined. It's a simple fact that air flowing over the structure of a plane produces an aerodynamic force, which either assists flight, such as lift, or hinders it, such as drag, or a variable mixture of the two forces. Drag is the air resistance all planes encounter as they meet the airflow, and its force acts in the opposite direction to the route of travel. Drag, in a sense, holds the plane back – and the more drag, the more energy required to overcome it.

Thrust is provided by one or more sources of power, such as a piston or a jet engine, or (in the case of a glider) by the energy derived from being hauled into the air by a ground-based winch or towed behind a propeller-driven plane. Thrust must balance drag for the plane to fly, and so it pays to reduce drag as much as possible with a streamlined design, as well as by cleaning and polishing the plane, so as to reduce the power required. A smaller powerplant is usually lighter, consumes less energy, creates less drag and places less strain on the airframe.

Lift and the Angle of Attack

Now we can examine the way in which a wing creates a variable amount of lift according to the angle at which it meets the airflow, known as the angle of attack. It does not matter which way up you are when you are flying: the wing always has an angle of attack in relation to the air flowing over it. The best way to illustrate this concept in a simple, practical sense is to show how a plane maintains level flight (does not climb or descend) when it slows down or speeds up.

Maintaining Height when Slowing Down

Most planes, when travelling at their cruising speed, are designed to fly more or less horizontally in line with the fuselage. In order to slow down in level flight you have to reduce the thrust from the engine, but as you slow down, the lift produced by the wings decreases; so, if you don't want to descend, you need to increase the lift. Pulling back on the control column raises the nose and inclines the wings upwards, thus increasing the angle of the wings to the airflow and providing more lift [4]. From the cockpit this is a strange sensation at first, seeing the nose high and yet the plane not gaining height.

See how steep the downwash from the wing is in diagram 4. This attitude is maintained by keeping the control column held back, deflecting the elevator upwards. Balancing lift from the wings and an appropriate thrust setting from the engine to maintain height at slow speed takes practice: if the nose is too high, the wing will stall and lose lift, and lowering the nose at this power setting will cause the plane to descend.

Maintaining Height when Speeding Up

Let's assume you are flying at a slow speed with a high angle of attack, maintaining height. If you want to increase your speed, you must apply more power. However, if you

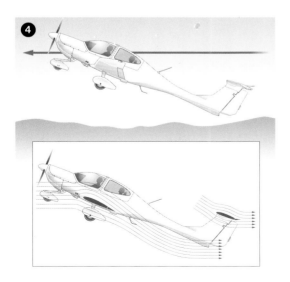

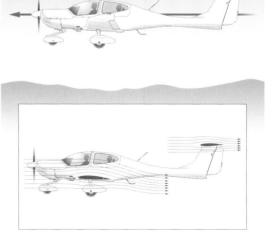

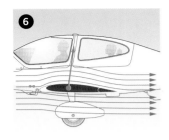

maintain the high angle of attack, the increase in speed will create more lift and you will climb. You must, therefore, reduce the angle of attack to stay at the same height. Ease the control column forward to lower the nose: the plane accelerates further and the wing is now at a lower angle of attack (the wing does not need to push the air down so sharply as speed increases). When you increase power and maintain height, the plane speeds up. At a cruise power-setting the wing still has an angle of attack, albeit a small one: it still needs to push the air down in order to fly.

If you want to increase power to a maximum, you will have to push the control column forward again to prevent a climb. When maintaining height at cruise and higher speeds, the nose of the plane points level too, and on some types the fuselage points well below the horizon, which is good for forward visibility. At maximum speed when maintaining height the wing needs only a very small angle of attack to create the necessary lift to support the plane [5]. From diagram 5, you can see that the downwash is slight, and the elevator is in a neutral position.

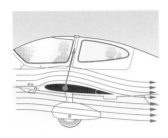

Stalling at Slow Speed

If the angle of attack becomes too pronounced, the flow of air over the wing is unable to remain streamlined or smooth, following the profile of the aerofoil [6]. As soon as the wing reaches this critical angle of attack, the airflow over and behind the wing becomes turbulent (this is the buffet you feel through the controls as the turbulent air encounters the tail surfaces). As the airflow breaks down, lift is lost and the wing stalls. The four stages in diagram 6 also show how the centre of lift force (known as the centre of pressure) – represented by the red dot on the wing – moves first of all forward in slow flight and then back in the stall. This causes a change in the longitudinal balance of the plane, creating a downward pressure on the nose in the stall.

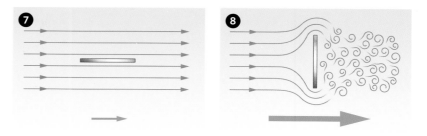

Drag

Drag is an aeronautical term for the air resistance experienced by a plane as it moves through the air. In its simplest expression, compare the flow of air over two plates, the first lying parallel to the airflow **[7]**, the second at a 90° angle **[8]**.

In the first case, there is little resistance to the airflow, and any drag that does exist is caused by the air colliding with the edge of the plate. As the air has not separated from the surface of the plate, drag is low. If the plate is turned to a 90° angle against the airflow, it's clear that the air cannot pass over the plate in a streamlined or smooth manner and drag is high. In fact, the airflow separates from the surface of the plate and forms turbulence in its wake. Reducing drag is, not surprisingly, a major preoccupation of plane designers and is particularly in evidence in more modern planes as technological advances in aeronautical computer modelling allow designers to follow drag patterns around a plane throughout its speed range in minute detail.

The amount of drag produced by a plane varies across its speed range, but also depends on other factors. A well-designed aerofoil should provide minimum drag on average for the speed range, and characteristics of the plane, when the airflow is streamlined. Even when an aerofoil is parallel to the airflow **[9]**, there is always a small amount of drag evident in the form of vortices in the trail or wake of the wing – and indeed the entire plane leaves behind it a trail of disturbed air, also known as its wake, which can be reduced by streamlining the plane. However, as soon as the airflow over the surface of the wing is disturbed **[10]**, turbulence is created and drag increases substantially. This is what happens when a wing is presented to the airflow at a high angle of attack and the airflow separates from the surface of the wing, causing it to stall.

Drag also increases if the shape or surface condition of the wing and airframe change. If a plane flies into damp or wet freezing air, ice tends to form on the airframe.

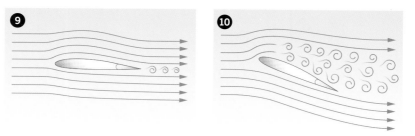

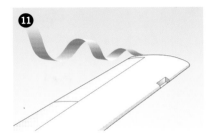

Ice changes the shape of the surface it clings to and is also heavy, so the plane will not only experience a reduction in lift but also an increase in weight and drag. All-weather planes, such as commercial airliners, are equipped with effective anti-ice systems on the wings, tail and engines. Less significant from a safety perspective is the increased drag from dirt and other deposits. But for high-performance gliders, cleaning off the squashed insects from the leading edge of a wing increases lift efficiency and speed, and every second counts in a soaring competition.

Efficient low-drag airframe and wing design has evolved rapidly, not only as a result of advances in aeronautical technology and engineering but also as a result of the use of new materials such as composites, allowing the creation of smoother surfaces and profiles. An example of this can be seen on the wings of an increasing number of planes, as airliners, business jets, light trainers and gliders sprout wing extensions, known generically as winglets. Without these winglets **[11]**, the airflow passing over the wing at the wingtip spills off to the side, and the upper and lower airflows combine to form a twisting mass of air known as a 'wingtip vortex'. Vortices occur along the entire trailing edge of a wing, but the wingtip vortex is the most powerful, especially when the wing is at a high angle of attack. You may have seen this in practice when an airliner approaches to land in moist air, leaving a trail of twisting condensation from the wingtips in its wake. Winglets, in principle, reduce the spillage or leakage of air around the wingtip, so that vortices are less powerful and drag is reduced **[12]**.

Thrust

Most light planes have an internal combustion engine or engines that drive a propeller to create thrust which either pulls you along or, in less common designs, pushes you. A propeller can also be driven by a jet engine, known as a jet turbine, which has become increasingly popular in general aviation, as well as in air transportation that does not require the higher speeds afforded by pure jet planes. A propeller becomes inefficient and ineffective at providing thrust beyond 350 knots (650 kph). Pure jet propulsion (without a propeller) is intrinsically simple and involves the compression and combustion of an air and fuel mix which is directed aft (towards the tail) to provide thrust. Jet propulsion permits high-speed as well as supersonic flight (travelling faster than the speed of sound). Traditionally the preserve of high-speed military planes and airliners, many new jet-propelled light business jets and personal jets are in development and production.

Flight Controls

All planes are manoeuvred (to make a turn, climb or descend) using three movable control surfaces: elevator, ailerons and rudder. The pilot controls their movement from the cockpit, either by hand flying (with direct inputs from hands and feet) or by instructing the autopilot (which generally involves turning or sliding small knobs or switches). The actual process of moving the control surfaces is often direct, as in most light planes where the controls in the cockpit are linked by cables (typically the elevator and rudder) or rods (usually the ailerons). In more complex planes, which are often heavier or faster, or both, some or all of these flight control surface movements are power-assisted, generally by hydraulic means. In more recent designs the link between the pilot and the control surface actuators is electronic (fly-by-wire) with mechanical back-up.

As the flight controls are moved, they change the pattern of the airflow over the aerofoil, increasing or reducing lift, and causing an overall movement of the plane – thus in a real sense acting as destabilizers. The coordinated, smooth movement of the three sets of flight control surfaces ensures stable and comfortable manoeuvring: on each wing there is an aileron to control rolling movement; the elevator and rudder are located on the tail and control movement in pitch, and directional control in yaw, respectively.

The flight controls in the cockpit are in principle identical in the majority of planes, but not all planes handle in the same way! You push or pull the control column (or yoke) to control pitch with the elevator, and deflect the column from side to side (rotate the yoke) to control roll with the ailerons, and you can of course make control column movements that combine pitch and roll. The rudder pedals are not just a foot rest, but also move the rudder for directional control in yaw.

Elevator

When you push the control column forward, the tail-mounted elevator deflects down, changing the profile of the horizontal stabilizer: the airflow is deflected downwards, causing additional lift and the tail to rise **[13]**. The nose of the plane therefore goes down. Conversely, pull back on the control column, and the elevator deflects up, guiding the airflow up, and causing the tail to drop and the nose to rise **[14]**. This becomes instinctive for most people! The further you push or pull, the greater the pitching movement, which pivots about the plane's centre of gravity. If you were to lift a plane up on a cable from its centre of gravity – indicated in illustrations 13, 14 and 18 (overleaf) by a pin-wheel symbol – it would hang and balance level.

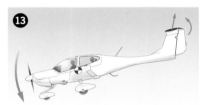

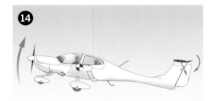

Elevators vary in shape and in surface area, especially in relation to the size of the horizontal stabilizer, to which the elevator is normally hinged. In simple terms, the larger the elevator, the more pitching force is available. Most elevators also have an additional movable control surface, or pair of surfaces, known as a trim tab, to allow the pilot to remove the adverse forces he feels through the column at different speeds and attitudes of flight.

Ailerons

Like all flight control surfaces ailerons deflect the airflow, reducing or increasing lift, and therefore lowering or raising a wing respectively. When you move the control column to one side, the aileron on each wing deflects, but in opposite directions, and the plane rolls [15]. The ailerons are located on the trailing edge of the wings, usually outboard; the further away they are from the plane's centre of gravity, the more effective the rolling force.

Imagine you are looking straight ahead from the cockpit. If you move the control column to the left, the aileron on the right wing deflects down, guiding the airflow downwards and thus pushing the wing up [16]; at the same time its counterpart on the left wing deflects upwards, guiding the airflow upwards and reducing the lift on that wing [17]. In level flight the ailerons lie parallel with the wing, but often there may be slight imperfections in their shape which can cause a disturbance to the airflow. For example, the plane might roll slowly one way or the other when the control column is released. For this reason ailerons on light planes are sometimes fitted with an adjustable trim tab on their trailing edge. Unless the plane has aileron trim controls, this tab can only be adjusted on the ground. As with all control surfaces, the larger the ailerons, the faster the plane responds in roll, which is why very dynamic aerobatic planes have large ailerons in proportion to the surface area of the wing.

Rudder

Most planes, unless they have a twin-tail configuration, are fitted with one rudder attached to the vertical stabilizer which is moved from side to side by applying pressure to the rudder pedals. The rudder primarily allows the pilot to yaw the nose of the plane horizontally to one side, pivoting about the centre of gravity.

Push the left rudder pedal and the rudder deflects left, so that the deflection of the airflow pushes the tail right **[18]**. As the nose turns to the left, the right wing moves faster than the left wing, thus creating more lift; as a result, unless the ailerons are deflected, the right wing will rise and the plane will start to roll to the left. For most flying, the rudder is used for keeping a plane in balance directionally in level flight and particularly when turning. This is described more fully in Chapter 2.

Effectiveness of Flight Controls

As we have seen, you can increase the effectiveness of a flight control surface by increasing its size, or rather its surface area in relation to the aerofoil to which it is attached. But it's also worth remembering that control surfaces are more or less effective in relation to the increased or reduced airflow over their surface. At slow speeds and with a reduced airflow, controls feel sloppy, are less responsive to the touch and require larger movements. At high speeds, controls are more effective, requiring small movements, but can feel heavy due to the greater effort needed to overcome the high-speed flow of air.

2 Let's Go Flying

Pre-flight Checks and Start-up

Your flight begins long before you climb into the plane. For the most enjoyable and safe flight, thorough planning and preparation are essential.

Before you are ready to fly, you need to ask yourself a number of questions:

- Most importantly, are you fit? Flying in a poor physical or mental state is unacceptable.
- Is the weather suitable for flying – or, rather, for the type of flying you have in mind? Most light planes are equipped to fly in cloud, but not in icing conditions. However, a pilot cannot enter cloud unless he has been trained and authorized to do so, and this includes approaching to land with reference to instruments.
- Is the plane serviceable?
- Is your personal paperwork in order and up to date? This includes flying licence, certificate of currency and medical certificate – and, if you own a plane, its certification, including proof of airworthiness and insurance documents.

In addition to the paperwork, each pilot gathers a uniquely personal selection of flying essentials, made up of equipment and other sundries. Legally you must carry an up-to-date flying chart as these are frequently revised to incorporate new radio frequencies and airspace alterations. An airfield guide is a really useful handbook, showing the layout of airfields, radio frequencies and other services. A knee board (available in many sizes) may also prove its worth as many cockpits are cramped and it's a good idea to keep pens and papers secure and to hand.

Check you have the most up-to-date charts and airfield information every time you fly.

Assess Flying Conditions

At the airfield visit the operations centre and take a moment to establish the conditions and state of the airfield itself. Is it dry? If you use grass surfaces, note their condition. Look at the windsock to confirm the runway in use, and also the force of the wind. Ask operations staff and local pilots what the flying conditions are like, and if there are any local or regional specific conditions you should be aware of – such combined knowledge is invaluable, especially if you are a visiting pilot. Consult the weather forecast for your planned area of flying, and confirm that there are no flying restrictions or warnings in place. All this information is available on the internet too, but bear in mind how fast weather conditions can change, so it's worth double-checking immediately before you fly. Once airborne you can also radio to ask what the weather is like at your destination or diversion airfield.

Before you walk to the plane, notify the airfield of your intentions – known as 'booking out' – and file a flight plan if you want to cross water and/or international borders.

Take in the Bigger Picture

On your approach, look at the overall state of the plane. Does it look level, with all tyres inflated? Is there anything that strikes you as odd or missing? Are there pools of fluid or any signs of staining under the plane, indicating a leak of engine oil or hydraulic fluid? Avgas fuel leaks leave a blue/green stain. Is this a good position to start the engine, so you don't damage or distress other planes with your propwash? Is the ground firm? Loose stones or debris could damage your propeller. If there's much of a breeze, are you facing into wind, or could you manhandle the plane into wind?

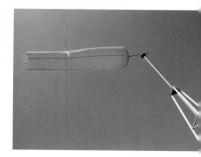

Now leave your flying gear in the plane. As you're doing so, check that the battery is not flat by flicking the master switch on, and cast an eye over the fuel gauges. Then turn the master switch off. You must not rely on the fuel gauges, which are notoriously inaccurate, so make a visual check of the fuel in the tanks on your walk around. Remove any control locks in the cockpit, which stop the control surfaces from flapping around in the wind, and then walk around the plane, clockwise, starting and finishing at your point of access. Follow your external checklist, and be sure to remove covers, blanks and pins. This may seem obvious but you'd be surprised at how many accidents have been caused by pilots attempting to take off with covers, and even tow arms, still in place! As you walk, consider the sobering fact that this is the last chance you have to check over the state of a machine you are about to rely on in the air. So take your time and be methodical.

Familiarize Yourself with the Cockpit

When you are happy that everything is as it should be, examine the cockpit and seating area for loose articles and secure any luggage or articles not needed in flight. Check that the seat belts are in good working order and the seat is secure on its runners or mount. Climb in and, where possible, adjust the seating position so that you are able to look out easily – forward and to the sides. Before you strap in, you should make sure that you have your headset, charts and flight planning document to hand. Secure your seat belt and then begin the pre-flight and engine-start checklist. You may need to listen out on the airfield information frequency for the latest observations and instructions for departure and landing, and you may also need to call on the radio to request start. Even if you have permission to start, you must

You're about to take to the skies, so make sure your external checks are thorough and methodical.

always look all around you and then call out loudly and clearly 'clear prop'.

The moment the engine starts, monitor the oil pressure gauge to ensure that, within a short time, you have a healthy reading (normally in the green). If you are in any doubt, shut down immediately and investigate. Now that the engine is running, look left and right and check the brakes are holding. There's usually so much noise that you may not notice you're creeping forward. Switch on the avionics master switch, put on your headset and check the radios are operational while you wait for the engine to warm up.

Sensations

Noise *Engine* There's an instant transition from silence to the cacophony of engine and propeller.

Feel *Brakes* Make sure you don't roll forward on starting.

Focus *Awareness* Be alert. You need to monitor engine instruments carefully, and yet be aware of what's going on outside. Remember that the engine is noisy, so maintain a good lookout.

Communication and Navigation

For many training and low-hour pilots, radio communication (known as radio telephony) and navigation present perhaps the most stressful aspect of aviation. The reasons are clear: it's embarrassing to come across as incompetent on the radio, and it's deeply distressing to be lost! You only have to listen to the communications between airline or military pilots and their controllers to feel inadequate. It's all so succinct, sharp and fast, like a foreign, acronym-packed technical language in shorthand. As for navigation, at first glance the aeronautical charts look completely alien as they're extremely colourful and full of strange and seemingly abstract numbers, codes and lines – bewilderingly different from a road map or atlas. With preparation, practice and good coaching, you'll soon discover that radio work and navigation are a rewarding challenge. There's something very satisfying about mastering the specific phraseology and making effective, concise and clear radio calls.

There's a simple rule of priorities when you're busy in a small cockpit, attempting to multi-task:

- *Always aviate first* Fly the plane safely and effectively, including steering clear of bad weather.
- *Communicate second* If in doubt talk to an air traffic service.
- *Navigate last* Light planes don't travel very fast, giving you time to assess the situation.

Master Your Radio Technique

The international language of the air is English. Most powered planes carry one or more VHF (Very High Frequency) radios, which are easy to operate and work on a 'line of sight' principle (you can't talk to an airfield if there's anything in the way, such as a mountain). Each air traffic service on the ground has a different radio frequency, which

It's all about practice. Pretty soon you'll be able to communicate and navigate with confidence.

is manually entered into the plane's radio by turning knobs or pressing buttons. Most planes are also equipped with a transponder; this radio device transmits a signal to a radar operator, allowing you to be identified in the air.

A light and comfortable headset combines a pair of earphones for listening and a boom microphone for transmitting. Most small passenger or training planes are fitted with an intercom, also connected to the headset, enabling pilots to communicate easily with each other in the cockpit. Some cockpits are really noisy, not only from the engine, but also from the airflow, and the padded earphones of the headset provide a degree of noise insulation. For increased comfort, active noise reduction (ANR) headsets are available, and for improved head protection military-style helmets (again, with or without ANR) are ideal for planes with an open cockpit or no roll-over crash protection, such as biplanes, warbirds and many aerobatic types.

Radio communications need to be clear and concise at all times, as any confusion in a message can have

tragic results, particularly in a busy airspace. This need for clarity is the responsibility of not only the pilot, but also the ground-based controller or adviser.

Only one person can transmit at one time on a frequency. To do this, you must press a transmit button, usually located on the throttle or control column, and then speak your message into the boom microphone clearly, succinctly, confidently and at an even pace. Then release the transmit button and wait for an answer.

Radio Tips

There are three secrets to an effective and successful radio technique:
- *Think first* What are you going to say? If necessary, write down the key data on your knee pad.
- *Listen out* You can't transmit over another call in progress. Wait for a gap in calls (this is not easy in a busy airspace) before transmitting.
- *Take notes* Write down any instructions or information you receive or want to communicate on your knee pad. You'll be amazed how quickly you forget numbers such as runway headings, radio frequencies and transponder codes. It's not easy to fly, think, write and speak all at once, and even less so when the plane is bouncing around in turbulence.

Radios are used in flight for many different reasons: to communicate instructions (e.g. a ground-based controller giving clearance to take off), advice (e.g. a pilot notifying a controller of his position) or warnings (e.g. turbulence on an approach to land by either a pilot to a controller, or a controller to pilots), and ultimately to request assistance in the event of an urgent problem (in which case you call PAN, PAN, PAN) or an emergency (which is announced by transmitting MAYDAY, MAYDAY, MAYDAY). There is a dedicated frequency for urgent and emergency calls, but

if there's no time to change frequency a distress call has priority over all calls, and all support and assistance will be given to the airman in trouble.

Finally, it's worth remembering that some planes operate without a radio at all, such as vintage types, and that a pilot may experience radio failure or radio confusion (turning down the volume control, for example). Some pilots use a radio as little as absolutely necessary, so whilst you should be alert and listening to the radio to monitor the position and activity of other planes, there's no substitute for a good lookout at all times.

Know Your Way Around

The view of the ground from the cockpit is both exciting and disturbing: you get to see the landscape from a new perspective, but at the same time it feels like you're entering the unknown. Most people are familiar with road navigation, and some of the generic navigation skills cross over, such as the sun rising in the east and setting in the west, but in the air there are no roads or road signs, and you can't stop to ask for directions – except, of course, by radio or landing. Where permitted, you can also fly directly in a straight line from A to B, and there are no speed limits (except for going very fast, such as supersonic) and no traffic police as such, although you are liable to be prosecuted by the Aviation Authorities if you stray into a no-go area (the airspace of a major international airport, for example). Running out of fuel, however, takes on a new meaning as pulling over is not an option; a thorough understanding of the fuel capacity of a plane and its consumption is crucial. And of course it's important to know where you are in relation to potential obstructions, whether man-made or natural.

It's also vital to know exactly where you can fly. The sky is divided into both horizontal and vertical zones that aim to separate safely light planes from intensive aerial activity, whether commercial airliners or military operations. Maps specifically created for light plane navigation show clearly – once you can read them – where you can and cannot

fly. Large areas around international airports and military air bases can be accessed or crossed only by obtaining permission (by radio or by prior telephone contact), and the sky between international airports is linked by airways at different levels, which can only be entered by pilots with specific qualifications and in planes with appropriate radio navigation and identification aids. Yes, in many heavily populated areas the airspace is very crowded with restrictions, and there is a tendency for this to increase as airline traffic grows. But there are routes around and sometimes through these areas, and good training and methodical flight planning will ensure you arrive safely.

Don't Rely on GPS

During training, the first skills to acquire relate to handling the plane safely, largely within the home airfield area. The second key set of skills concern navigation (including meteorology, an understanding of weather for airmen). Light plane navigation has been revolutionized over recent years by the introduction of small, lightweight, easy-to-use GPS (Global Positioning System) units, which are either fixed into the panel or removable and mounted on a bracket in the cockpit. All are largely intuitive to operate and, once

powered up, will fix a position over or on the earth using satellite data. When you key in your destination, the unit draws a line for you to follow and continuously guides you to that point, regardless of weather conditions. Your position is pinpointed on a screen, and the information is usually map-based. The trend is for these GPS units to include more and more information, such as terrain, weather and instrument landing information.

Despite these reliable devices, you need the fundamental skills of navigational awareness and route planning to be a safe pilot. Once you have a licence, however, a GPS is a wonderful back-up to these skills, as well as acting as a safety device by reducing cockpit workload. This should, in theory, give you more time not only to enjoy the flight, but crucially to spend more time looking out for conflicting traffic.

Your training to be a pilot navigator involves learning how to use the cockpit direction indicator (in combination with the cockpit compass) and to monitor your time airborne with a watch, along with other various essentials: the appropriate aeronautical map, a navigation computer (like a slide rule of old), a scale ruler and protractor, pens and pencils, flight log forms (in essence a spreadsheet of

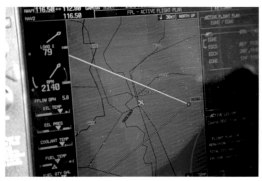

flight planning data), and a flight information publication showing airfield and airspace details. In addition to these hand-powered devices, you'll also need access to accurate weather forecasting too, much of which is now web-based and free. Most single-engine light planes cruise at less than 130 knots (240 kph), and the direction and strength of the wind therefore have a major impact. Of course, it's important to avoid (or not fly in) bad weather until you have gained an instrument rating qualification allowing you to fly in very poor visibility or in cloud.

Your navigation test for a flying licence requires you to know how to prepare, plan and fly from one airfield to another and land there, with no help from a GPS. It's a great feeling to plan and fly a trip accurately and safely using no electronic equipment except the direction indicator and perhaps your watch.

Sensations

Noise *Radio* You'll be amazed at the contrast between busy radio exchanges at an airfield and the relatively low radio activity away from controlled airspace.

Feel *Organization* Time spent organizing your flight planning on the ground will repay tenfold in the confined cockpit.

Focus *Aviate* Your first priority is to maintain safe control of your plane and to avoid other planes, no matter how busy you are communicating and navigating in the cockpit.

Navigation is about spatial awareness, linking what you see outside with what your instruments and map tell you.

Taxi and Pre-takeoff

You'll often see piston-engine planes sitting after start-up with their engines running. Generally, the pilot is not only making sure that he has been through all the start-up checks, but also that the engine is warm enough for taxi and power checks before takeoff.

Once you've completed your start-up checks, it's time to radio the tower and ask for assistance in three ways:

- Firstly, to check that the radio is functioning, ensuring that you can be heard and vice versa.
- Secondly, to confirm which runway is in use, the correct taxi route to that runway, and the sea-level pressure-setting to dial into the altimeter, which will show you at a glance that the altimeter is reading accurately.
- And thirdly, if necessary, to ask permission to taxi.

Before you release the brakes, have a good look around you and, if it's all clear, reduce power to minimum, release the brakes, and increase the power smoothly. After a metre or so, apply the brakes against the power to test them. Once you're rolling along, you will gain momentum and will therefore need to reduce power. When you want to stop, close the throttle completely as you apply the brakes.

Taxi the plane at walking pace, keeping a good lookout. You'll need to check the operation of the rudder and flight instruments as you taxi, so look ahead and select an unobstructed area where you can turn left and right, ensuring that the rudder is fully free from one side to the other. In the cockpit check that the attitude indicator isn't moving. When you go left, the slip ball moves or skids right, the turn indicator shows a left turn and the direction indicator and standby compass should decrease in

One of the most important checks before takeoff is making sure that all controls move freely.

heading. The opposite indications will be seen in a turn to the right.

Continue taxiing to the holding point of the runway in use, where you will complete your pre-takeoff checks. Signboards near the runway threshold indicate in shorthand the runway compass heading, such as 28 for 280° – or its reciprocal (10 for 100°). As you approach the holding point, reduce power to slow down and then turn the plane as much as possible into the wind (so that the engine is less likely to overheat during power checks) – usually this means you will be at an angle across the taxiway but short of the holding point. Close the throttle, stop, engage the parking brake and then set power to idle.

Check, and Check Again

Your pre-takeoff checks are really important as this is your last opportunity to assess the plane's condition and the engine's performance on the ground. You must follow the pre-takeoff checklist for your type of plane, which will include the following:

- Set trim and flaps for takeoff.
- You should have already checked that the flight instruments worked when you were taxiing. Now also make sure the direction indicator is aligned with the compass, and the airspeed indicator reads zero.
- Check that the engine temperatures and pressures are normal. Make sure the parking brake is set and then increase power to the recommended power-check setting to establish that the engine is

functioning within the recommended limits. With a high power-setting on the ground, keep an eye out for the plane creeping forward against the brakes, or slipping if you are on wet grass.

- Make sure you're strapped in securely, and that the doors or hatches are closed and locked.
- Switch on visibility lights, such as wingtip strobes.
- Ensure that you, as pilot in command, are content that the controls move freely and are not restricted in any way.

All set? One last safety check before you call the tower to request permission for departure: turn your plane around on the taxiway at the holding point so you can see if there is any traffic approaching to land on the runway in use. All clear? Then it's time to call for departure....

Sensations

Noise *Engine* Has a regular beat once warmed up. Does it sound smooth?

Radio *Transmissions of other pilots and controllers* Be aware of who's about and what's happening at the airfield.

Feel *Controls* Keep a loose grip on the controls, and feel for the toe pressure required to apply the brakes.

Smell *Engine* You'll probably be able to smell the warming engine, especially after the power check. A warm and agreeable aroma is good, but a burning smell at any time is a cause for concern.

Always double-check that the approach path is clear of landing planes before you enter the runway for takeoff.

Takeoff

Before you leave the holding point and taxi onto the runway in use, always double-check that the runway itself, and the airspace all around you, is clear. This is vitally important, even if you have received clearance to enter the runway. Some planes are not radio-equipped – known as 'non-radio traffic' – and may be landing. Occasionally pilots may be confused and approach to land from the opposite direction or on a diagonal runway. And if a plane is making an emergency landing, it may appear without warning. Whatever the situation, landing traffic always has right of way over takeoff traffic.

Line Up and Start to Roll

Once you leave the holding point, taxi without delay to line up at the threshold, which is usually at the end of the runway. You may have to backtrack to do so. Don't waste runway: there's nothing more useless on takeoff than runway behind you. Make sure that you are on the centre line of the runway, and that the nose wheel or tail wheel is straight so that you don't have to make any steering adjustments when you start to roll. Apply the brakes to hold the plane steady as you make one last full and free check of the flight controls, confirm the engine temperatures and pressures are normal,

As you accelerate on takeoff, look ahead so that you can track the centreline accurately.

and then push the throttle steadily and progressively forward to full power. Don't rush this: count 'three bananas' as you do so and simultaneously release the brakes, letting your heels slide down the pedals to rest on the floor. Immediately glance at the engine power instruments to make sure the engine is developing full power.

When you start to move, and depending on the power of the engine, you'll experience a rush of sensations. It's really exciting! However, don't get so carried away with what's going on inside the cockpit that you don't pay due attention to the outside, or vice versa. You'll be working to keep the plane tracking straight with the rudder by looking ahead towards the end of the runway, whilst cross-checking the instruments to see that the engine is healthy and speed is increasing on

the airspeed indicator. Keep a light but confident touch on the controls, and you'll begin to feel them come alive.

Up, Up and Away

As you gather pace, protect the nose wheel by applying a little back pressure on the control column. This will take the weight of the engine off the nose and, as you approach takeoff speed, the plane is likely to want to fly. Ease back steadily on the control column, looking forward to see the nose rise, and feel the plane take to the air. It's crucial to maintain the best climb speed for the plane, although this varies from type to type. Don't let this put you off: with practice you'll soon learn to fly each type of plane by 'feel'. Start off by establishing a climb angle in relation to the horizon, looking ahead and over the nose to do so, and keep the plane at this attitude. If your airspeed is too high, pull back a little, which will raise the nose slightly and reduce your airspeed. If your airspeed in the climb is too low, ease the control column forward, which will lower the nose slightly and increase the airspeed. Keep the wings level with smooth, yet responsive side-to-side movements of the control column and prevent yaw with rudder pressure. At the best climb speed the controls feel less responsive and require more application than at cruise speed.

By the time you reach about 200 ft (60 m) and have established a steady climb, you can raise the undercarriage and flaps if appropriate. Some planes will sink for a short time after the takeoff flap is retracted, so resist the temptation to whip the flaps up as soon as you're airborne. Likewise, raising the undercarriage smartly after takeoff may make you feel sharp, but could compromise a safe landing if you experience an engine failure at this stage. Continue the climb, and maintain your scan of the vital instruments (airspeed, altimeter and engine gauges) whilst looking forward and, if possible, down and to the sides to see if you are tracking straight ahead in line with the runway. When you're approaching 500 ft (150 m), complete your after takeoff checks.

Caution

This first minute or two in the air is not only exhilarating but also the time when you need to be most attentive. It is very rare for a modern plane engine to fail, but if it does, lower the nose immediately to achieve the best glide speed. What you do next depends on how high you are when the engine fails. If you're less than 200 ft above the ground, land straight ahead – you may be able to do so on the runway or within the airfield, or select an open area straight ahead. Between about 200 ft and 500 ft in the air, land ahead or within 30° either side of your direction by making a gentle turn. Below 500 ft, never attempt to turn back as you won't have the height to do so. Above 500 ft, you're likely to have more time to turn further and to select an appropriate place to land, whether on the airfield or close by.

Sensations

Noise *Engine* At full power the engine will be at its noisiest. *Airflow* The rush of air over the airframe will become evident as you lift off.

Feel *Controls* At a very slow speed the controls are slack, and largely ineffective. They soon become responsive on takeoff. *Vibration* If on grass there are likely to be some bumps and thumps.

Focus *Ready to react* You're close to the ground and slow, so monitor the engine often, and be ready to act instantly should mechanical failure occur.

Climbing and Level Flight

When climbing, the nose of your plane may be inclined well above the horizon, leaving an entire area of sky obscured, both in front of you and below you. It's a really unsettling feeling, climbing without being able to see ahead, and you must therefore take positive action: every 500 ft (150 m) lower the nose slightly and then turn by about 10 to 15° either side of your climb-out direction. The change of direction is not an exact science, but a means of checking that there is no one ahead, and with practice can be done smoothly and, if you have passengers, rhythmically, so that they do not endure a roller-coaster ride. This technique should also be used in a descent to make sure the airspace ahead of your path is clear.

Decide on a Climb Rate

Once you're airborne, you can climb at different rates and speeds to suit your requirements at the time. If you want to climb as quickly as possible – known as the max rate climb – you need to push the throttle forward to achieve the maximum continuous power, then ease back on the control column to raise the nose above the horizon to the attitude recommended for the plane (usually between 10 and 30° up). Wait for the plane to decelerate and stabilize at the recommended max rate climb speed. Once you're settled in the climb, hold the column steady and then trim out the adverse forces on the control column with the elevator trim,

so that when you let go of the column at the maximum power setting the plane flies itself. When you need to change the power setting (to climb, descend, increase or reduce speed when level), first apply or reduce the power, then select the attitude in relation to the horizon, and finally trim out the control forces. This method takes practice, but after a while you'll find it becomes instinctive!

A max rate climb is ideal when you don't need to go anywhere but want to reach a suitable height, say 5,000 to

Most small planes can be flown with a light touch. Feel for the control inputs you need to fly smoothly and accurately.

7,000 ft (1,500–2,100 m), as fast as possible to practise aerobatics, for example, or stall and spin recovery. The max climb rate of single-engine planes varies widely, from the genteel ascent of a classic biplane to the exhilarating zoom climb of a warbird or aerobatic machine. Most aerobatic planes, by their very nature, have a good power-to-weight ratio, and their max climb rates vary from 500 ft per minute to over 2,000 ft (600 m) per minute and more.

Avoid Engine Wear and Tear

In a climb, the more power at your command, the higher the nose attitude above the horizon. Consequently there's a reduction in airflow over the engine, which is already working hard and is likely to be getting hot. The result? The engine could potentially overheat, and there is an increased likelihood of engine wear. The solution is to let more air flow over the engine. To do this, you have two choices: lower the nose (so that the plane has a lower attitude) to reduce the rate of ascent, or reduce power and level off to let temperatures stabilize before you resume your max rate climb again.

Remember that the air temperature typically drops by about 3°C (5°F) per thousand feet, and so the air gets cooler the more you climb. The air also becomes increasingly thin the higher you get, reducing the amount of lift the wing generates, which needs to be balanced by more power from the engine. This helps to explain why propeller-engine light planes are most efficient at flying below 10,000 ft (3,000 m). Above 10,000 ft the air is

Scan the primary flight instruments repeatedly. They should confirm what you see outside!

so thin that it is recommended you breathe oxygen, which is carried in portable bottles on certain light planes such as fast touring types. It's important to realize that warmer weather also has a detrimental influence on a plane's rate of climb. Quite simply, warmer air is thinner and so yet again lift is reduced. Flying in a hot and high location is the worst combination – a mountainous desert region at the height of summer, for instance. Less lift means less payload can be carried. Manufacturers clearly state the climb performance of their planes at a variety of temperatures and heights, and it's important you consult these charts for the safe loading of a plane.

A reduced rate of climb, in which a plane travels at a higher speed but covers a greater horizontal distance as it gains height, is known as a cruise climb. In this case, you power up to either maximum continuous power or a reduced power setting to conserve engine life, set a lower nose attitude on the horizon (such as between 3 and 15° up), and then trim to maintain the cruise climb attitude. The ascent is more gentle, the view over the nose much improved, and the rate of climb more comfortable, particularly for passengers. In general the engine also receives an increased flow of air, which reduces the risk of overheating in the climb. It's important to continue to make periodic clearing turns, or a gentle weave, in the cruise climb as you will not be able to see other planes ahead and slightly below you.

Level Off Smoothly and in Stages

As you approach your chosen height to level off, anticipate the change in attitude of the plane. There are two considerations here: firstly, to level off accurately, usually in 1,000 or 500 ft (300 or 150 m) stages, such as 2,500 or 3,000 ft (750 or 900 m) rather than, say, 2,700 ft (825 m), which would be hard to fly with precision; and secondly, to make the transition smoothly so that neither you nor any passengers feel the push over as you move the column forward, which, if made forcefully, gives the unpleasant sensation of being lifted in your seat. The answer to both is to fly smoothly, and reduce the rate of the climb in advance – at between 300 and 150 ft (90 and 45 m) before your chosen height depending on your rate of climb – by easing the control column forward.

Select your level flight attitude by looking out to the horizon and using it as a guide by placing the nose, canopy or coming on the horizon (each type of plane has different visual cues to use), and to the side by adjusting the angle of the wingtips in relation to the horizon. Once flying level, the plane will accelerate, and you'll have to maintain a forward pressure on the column to stay level. When you reach your chosen cruise speed, reduce the power to the recommended cruise setting, let the plane settle, then

Look at the position of the wings and nose in relation to the horizon. It's easy to see at a glance if you are climbing, flying level or descending.

retrim away any pressure on the column with the elevator trim. Let go of the column, and the plane should fly level hands-free. With practice this sequence becomes instinctive and you can focus your attention on accurate, smooth flying whilst maintaining a good lookout. Now complete your cruise checks, which include engine settings, fuel level, a navigation update and, if required, a radio call to declare you have levelled off.

Stay Alert!

Level flight is certainly less busy than landing and takeoff, but at no time when airborne and in command should you reduce your heightened sense of awareness. One of the best ways to maintain an efficient, alert state is to combine a visual sweep of the cockpit instruments with a glance outside the plane. Look across the instruments from left to right, and then from right wingtip to left wingtip across the nose. If you can, look upwards too. And be sure to pause your gaze in roughly 30° segments, focusing on a distant object – otherwise your eyes will tend to rest somewhere in the middle distance, typically around 15–20 ft (5–6 m) from the cockpit.

At the same time you can also utilize all your senses, to feel, touch, smell and hear how your plane is performing. A smell of burning may come from a factory or farm on the ground below, or it could be an indication of something amiss with your plane. Is there an unusual vibration or a change in the feel of the controls? Or a change in the engine note without moving the throttle? Then it's time to look at the engine instruments and, if necessary, your plane's checklist if a fault is found. You can always land at your nearest airfield to trace a fault or a problem. Clearly it's much better and easier to land a controllable plane before a problem gets worse.

Sensations

Noise *Engine* Some planes are noisy when the engine is working at maximum continuous power and so you'll be relieved to pull the power back for the cruise!

Feel *Controls* When climbing at a slow speed, make small and coordinated control movements such as gentle turns.

Focus *Diversion* It's best to be aware at all times where the nearest suitable airfield is, and how far away it is.

Turning

Once a plane is flying straight and level, trim out any fore and aft control forces on the column. When you let go of the controls, you'll find that the plane, for the most part, wants to fly in a straight line. In reality very few light planes are perfectly balanced in level flight, and there is often a tendency, when you let go of the controls, for the plane to turn very slowly and gently. This is usually because the ailerons are slightly out of balance or trim. Most ailerons possess a fixed trimming tab at their trailing edge, which can be bent up or down, but only on the ground. It's not a sophisticated system! If, when straight, level and trimmed, on releasing the controls you start to turn dynamically and if it's wearisome holding the wings level, then you need to land and investigate the cause.

There are really two types of turns for most light planes: those that are gentle and require no extra application of power; and steeper turns, at an extreme angle (more than 50–60° for instance), which may mean that the plane needs all available power to remain at the same height in the turn. The aerodynamic explanation is really quite straightforward. When a plane is flying straight and level at a steady speed, all the lift is pulling vertically upwards and balances the plane's weight exactly, while thrust balances drag. As soon as you roll into the turn, the lift force is angled into the turn, reducing its vertical component (which keeps you at the same height). You require more lift to compensate: the vertical lift as before, and the lift to one side that pulls you towards the centre of the turn. You generate this extra lift by increasing the angle of attack of the wing (by pulling back on the column), and if necessary by applying power in order to maintain speed and, ultimately, height. This is because increasing the angle of attack also creates more drag, and so you need more power to maintain speed.

Check the Airspace Around You

Now let's look at a gentle turn, which is 30° or less of bank, also known as a medium turn. Before you start a turn, you should consider the airspace you are about to turn into or

towards. First and foremost, is it clear of other planes? This may seem a repetitive instruction (and it is!) but it is vitally important to keep an eye out at all times, particularly when you change direction – both before and during the turn. Before you turn, you've no idea what might be under (low-wing plane) or above (high-wing plane) the wing you are going to turn towards, and the moment you raise a wing to turn you will be blind to the outside of the turn. While in the turn, you must look at the direction you are turning towards as conflicting traffic may appear at any time. You must also check whether you are about to turn towards or into an area that requires permission to enter or is a prohibited area.

To check for other traffic before you start the turn, first look quickly in the direction of your turn and then look out to the opposite side. Continue your gaze across the front of your plane before looking once again in the direction of your turn. All clear? Then don't delay. Start your turn by moving the control column in the direction of the turn, applying a little rudder at the same time in the same direction in order to maintain balance. Too much rudder and you will skid the tail out of the turn; too little and you will slip into the turn.

As you turn, make sure you look not only at the position of the nose in relation to the horizon, but also all around for other traffic.

You want to use the rudder to guide the tail around the turn. Each plane handles differently and so, until you can sense a slipping or skidding turn by the way your body reacts (largely through your seat – either you're slipping inwards or skidding outwards), you can quickly glance down at the slip ball on the panel, which is usually found at the foot of the attitude indicator. When the plane is in balance the slip ball sits in the middle of the indicator; when the ball moves to the left, apply left rudder, and vice versa.

Practice Makes Perfect

Gauge the angle of the turn by looking at the angle at which the engine cowling or the coming cuts the horizon. In a side-by-side seating plane this is easier in a turn to the left as the pilot in command sits on the left. Once the turn or bank angle of no more than 30° is established, you'll need to do two things pretty much simultaneously. Centralize and ease back a little on the column: the plane will remain in the turn and maintain height. Why? If you maintained the sideways pressure on the column, you would continue to increase the angle of bank because the sideways pressure on the column is continuing to demand a roll response from

When turning, make small corrections with the controls to ensure that the plane remains in balance.

the plane, i.e. the aircraft keeps rolling (increasing its bank angle) about its fore and aft axis. If you return the column to the central position, the plane will stay at the bank angle reached. In practice, this becomes intuitive virtually straight away. By easing back a touch, you generate the lift you need to stay at the same height. As soon as you increase the lift, you increase the drag, and thus slow down. However, for most light planes in a medium turn this reduction in speed is only about 5 knots (9 kph) and you therefore won't need to increase power to compensate. There's no need to trim out the back force you are applying to the column, as a turn – unlike a steady state such as cruising – is only a short-term, and often variable manoeuvre.

Making adjustments to your level turn is easy. If you're climbing, either increase the angle of bank and/or ease forward on the column. If you are descending you may have applied too much bank or are not easing back on the column sufficiently. Keep in balance by applying rudder pressure to maintain the slip ball in the centre and a comfortable upright feeling in your seat. When you are ready to roll out straight and level, move the column away from the turn (in the opposite direction to the turn), balance with rudder to the same side and ease forward on the column. You might be a bit wobbly at first, but with practice you'll soon be flying into and out of turns like an airliner on autopilot!

Sensations

Noise *Engine* It's unlikely you'll increase power from a typical cruise setting to complete a medium turn.

Feel *Controls* In order to complete the turn accurately, you'll need to apply and finesse your control inputs throughout the turn. The secret is applying small movements smoothly.

Focus *Lookout* I've said it before and I'll say it again, and again and again. Keep your focus out of the cockpit for safe and accurate flying. You only need to glance at the engine and flight instruments from time to time.

Slow Flight and Stalling

During most of your flights, you'll most probably be speeding along at or near the cruise speed of the plane. Typically your cruise speed is a balance between economical fuel burn and a relatively stress-free engine power setting. At other times you need to fly slowly and safely. This is always the case just as you take off, as well as immediately before you land. It's very worthwhile to practise slow flight, and also stalling, at a safe height so that you are comfortable with your plane's controllability and familiar with the sensations – particularly understanding the boundaries between slow flight and the stall, when the wings lose lift. Make sure you know the basic stalling speed for your plane, as you will be flying slowly just above this speed. Exploring the flying characteristics of a plane is exciting as each one is different!

Slowly Does It

First of all look out ahead and to the sides for other planes, as you will be flying largely in a straight line at the same height for slow flight practice. It's a good idea, therefore, to make gentle weaving turns from time to time so that you can see what's under the nose. At cruising speed, reduce power and then ease back on the column in order to maintain level flight; then trim. The nose will assume a higher attitude above the horizon and the plane will slow down. Now reduce power again, ease back to maintain level flight and trim. You'll be flying along at a slower speed with a higher nose attitude than before. The controls will feel less responsive than in the cruise; try gentle inputs and you're likely to feel as though you're stirring slop in a bucket rather than flying a plane. This is because the airflow over the control surfaces has been reduced, making them less effective. Reduce power again and try to maintain height. Pretty quickly you'll reach a point where the plane barely maintains height at a slow airspeed as you're now at a high angle of attack, which creates a lot of drag.

Now, to slow down yet further but maintain height, you'll need to apply power and pull back gently on the column. Trim and now, at this slower speed with power on, make a turn. Look out for conflicting traffic and make a gentle turn, no more than 20–30° bank; you'll need to add power in the turn to maintain height and you'll find that now, although the ailerons feel sloppy, the rudder and elevator are more responsive. This is because the elevator and rudder are in the engine's slipstream, but the ailerons are not. Roll wings level, and then continue to reduce your speed, adding power to maintain height, until you reach full power and are flying along at the slowest possible speed. This will depend on the power of the plane's engine and the speed at which its wings stall. It is not a comfortable flight attitude: the nose is high, the engine is roaring and you'll be close to the stall, anywhere between 5 and 15 knots (9–28 kph) above the stall speed. In order to keep the slip ball in the centre (to fly straight), you'll also have to apply quite a lot of rudder. This is because of the sideways force exerted by the powerful slipstream over the tail, and this twisting flow of air is dominant at low speeds.

Slow flying really is a good exercise for improving your coordination and sensitivity to the plane's flying characteristics. However, don't stay there for long as the engine may overheat with so little cooling airflow, and you can't see anything ahead of you. Understand and remember that the plane is not highly controllable, and that you certainly don't want to fly like this for long too close to the ground. Recover by easing forward on the column, and the plane will accelerate immediately. Once at cruising speed, reduce power to the cruise setting and trim.

Recognize the Symptoms

There's nothing complicated about a stall, and recovery from a stall is straightforward. But, as with slow flight, being low and slow or low and stalled is not a good state of affairs as you will need airspace below you to recover. You must practise stalls at a safe height. When and why a plane stalls and sinks is easy to grasp; you practise stalls to be able to identify the cause, symptoms and results, and to recover from a stall with a minimum loss of height. This is because you are flying quite close to the stall at the time you are closest to the ground – during takeoff and landing. It's much better to know how your plane flies, and fly it accurately, smoothly and safely at all attitudes and speeds, so you can avoid a stall near the ground.

A plane will stall – or, rather, the wings will be in a stalled state – when the smooth flow of air over the wings becomes turbulent (see page 17), resulting in a reduction of lift and an increase in drag. The air becomes turbulent over a wing whenever it is presented to the airflow at such a high

angle of attack that the air cannot flow in a streamlined way over its surface. You, as pilot, increase the angle of attack by pulling back on the control column. It follows, therefore, that you could pull back and stall the wings irrespective of the airspeed, and that you could recover by easing or pushing forward the column to reduce the angle of attack.

The Basics of Stalling

Cause Too high an angle of attack.
Symptoms Shaking and shuddering, known as buffet, felt through the airframe and controls from the turbulent air.
Results The plane descends and the nose drops.
Solution Push forward the control column to reduce the angle of attack and regain flying speed.

Practise Entry and Recovery

The simplest stall practice focuses on recovering from a straight and level position at the basic stall speed, which varies according to the type of plane. Given that a plane can stall at any speed, what's a basic stall speed? This is the stall speed of your plane when it is at maximum weight, with the wings clean (no flaps extended), and flying straight and level with no power. This is an unlikely combination when taking off or landing, and so it's very important to practise stalling at various combinations of speeds, configurations and entry attitudes.

Here we'll look at a simple stall from straight and level flight, and recovering from the stall with and without the application of power, as the recovery principles apply to all stalls. As you are about to fly the plane to a stalled condition, and you're going to descend before recovery, you need to double-check that you and your plane are prepared and that the airspace around you is clear of traffic. Your plane's handbook contains a pre-stall checklist, and there's also a useful mnemonic that always helps you to be ready for stalls and other aerobatic or semi-aerobatic manoeuvres: HASELL.

- *Height* Sufficient to recover? Usually at least 3,000 ft (900 m) above the ground.
- *Airframe* Position of flaps or undercarriage as required?
- *Security* Seat belt or harness secure and tight, hatch(es) closed and secure, no loose articles in cockpit?
- *Engine* All indications within limits in the green (normal operating temperatures and pressures), fuel sufficient,

With power at idle when straight and level, you won't be able to maintain height – eventually the plane will stall.

At the onset of the stall you will have a high angle of attack and the nose will be above the horizon.

engine controls as recommended by the plane's manual?

- *Location* Away from towns, other airfields or restricted airspace and in good weather with a clear horizon?
- *Lookout* Make a clearing turn of either 2 x 90° (one way, then the other) or a 180° turn, and make sure you look beneath you as well as all around you. Once you've completed your lookout, start the stall entry immediately.

The stall entry and recovery are not a huge drama. From straight and level flight, note your height, reduce power and ease back on the column to maintain the same height; the angle of attack will increase. Reduce power steadily, all the way to idle and continue to pull back in order to try to maintain height. Keep the slip ball in the centre with rudder. Just as for slow flight without power, you'll feel the sloppy controls, less airflow noise and, as the stall approaches, some light buffet, and of course you will be in a high-nose attitude. Once you stall you'll experience a high rate of descent, and the nose will drop or a wing will drop, or both. To recover, reduce the angle of attack. How? By easing forward centrally on the control column: you will 'unstall' the wings, the buffet will cease and the airspeed will increase, and you will be in a shallow dive. Ease out of the dive, applying power once you've placed the nose on the horizon, and you'll soon establish straight and level cruise speed. Look at the altimeter: you've probably lost about 150–250 ft (45–75 m) stalling and recovering.

You see? Not a problem, but not good if you're near the ground. This is why you also need to practise recovering from a stall with power. In between practice stalls complete the lookout again, and then level out and reduce power but maintain height (note this) as before. This time, once you feel the stall, recover by easing forward centrally on the column whilst applying full power in one steady movement. Maintain balance by using rudder to keep the slip ball centred. You'll speed up more rapidly; you can therefore ease back on the column more quickly to establish level flight. Look at the altimeter: with practice, height loss for a powered recovery can be less than 50 ft (15 m).

Sensations

Noise *Airflow* It's very quiet when you are flying slowly, or stalling without power. Make a mental note of how quiet it is as this is the time you are likely to be near the stall.

Feel *Controls* They are floppy at low speeds and you'll need to make firm, positive and smooth movements when required.

Focus *Lookout* Not only should you be looking out for other traffic, but you must also be aware of your position. Know the direction to your airfield, and be sure you are outside restricted airspace.

Descending and Arriving at an Airfield

How do you want to descend: quietly and slowly, or quickly? Fundamentally there are two ways to descend: without power or with power. In the first instance, with the engine throttled back to idle, the plane glides down. In the second, keeping some or all of the power on that you have been using for cruising, you are able to descend more quickly at a shallow angle, known as a cruise descent. There's no rule for the use of either technique, unless you experience engine failure, of course, in which case gliding is your only option! In reality, engine failure is an extremely rare occurrence.

In normal flight the way you descend is largely intuitive, and you can match your rate of descent and your speed in a wide variety of combinations according to your needs. A cruise descent is ideal if you're changing height on a cross-country flight. If you're descending over an airfield, making ready to land, glide down either without power or with just a trickle of power applied.

Whichever approach you choose, don't continue in a straight line for an extended period as you cannot see beneath you. Make weaving turns not only during your descent but also before you begin a descent.

Glide Descent or Cruise Descent?

Each plane has a best glide speed, which gives the most efficient glide angle for maximum distance covered without power. Gliding below this speed with a high angle of attack creates more drag and results in a quicker descent. Pushing the column forward to speed up beyond the best glide speed has the same end result: you'll accelerate but also descend more quickly.

As you approach your destination airfield, keep a sharp lookout for other traffic. Once over the airfield, confirm the direction of the landing runway. Fly an accurate circuit, and complete your checks thoroughly.

There's also another glide speed that's useful if you want to stay up for as long as possible when gliding: the best gliding endurance speed. This is usually about 25% less than the best glide speed. Refer to the manufacturer's handbook for these gliding speeds.

The majority of light planes are powered by air-cooled piston engines. Gliding a plane with the engine at idle cools the powerplant – and, unless your plane is fitted with flaps or gills that control the flow of air over the engine, you may well cool it too rapidly, known as shock cooling. This causes unnecessary stress to the engine, as well as fouling the plugs. The solution is to apply about 50% power for about 5 seconds every 1,000 ft (300 m) of descent in a glide.

To glide down from a straight and level cruise, make your clearing weave and then slowly pull the power all the way back to idle (you may need to change other engine controls too, depending on the type of plane). Always try to treat the engine with sensitivity as it will last longer and be more reliable. Keep straight by applying rudder to keep the slip ball central, and as the speed drops, ease back on the column. When you reach best glide speed, ease forward slightly on the column to maintain a stable attitude for this speed. The nose should be positioned low on the horizon. Trim. Every 500 ft (150 m) make weaving turns to check the area hidden under the nose for other planes.

In the cruise descent you are able to use power to control your rate of descent accurately. As always before a descent, check the area ahead of you for other planes by weaving, and then pull back on the throttle so that you maintain some power. The nose will drop. Once at a shallow attitude below the horizon, ease back on the control column to maintain this angle and trim. If you need to increase the rate of descent without speeding up too much, reduce power, ease forward on the control column to maintain the same speed, then trim; to reduce the rate of descent, increase power, ease back on the control column to raise the nose and maintain the same speed, and trim. Don't forget to make a weaving turn every 500 ft. If you're descending at low power, as with the glide you may need to apply power to keep the engine warm and clear the plugs.

Follow the Visual Circuit

The sky around an airfield is often busy. Airfields are not only places for landing and takeoff, but are also, where permitted, points to fly to and over during navigation exercises. You are more likely, therefore, to encounter planes at different heights and directions near an airfield. It is also a time when you as pilot are likely to be at your busiest, preparing for arrival or departure and focusing on flying safely, and when you are closest to the ground – so you need to be doubly alert!

At most airfields the landing and takeoff traffic use the same runway, and it is not safe practice to land on a runway occupied by other planes. It follows, therefore, that the preoccupation of arriving and departing pilots, and airfield traffic controllers where relevant, is to maintain safe and efficient spacing between the planes using the airfield. This is seen most dramatically at a busy commercial airport where the sky is full of landing and departing airliners and other traffic in a seemingly never-ending cycle of highly controlled activity. At the other extreme, many smaller airfields are not controlled airspace, and each plane is responsible for separation from other airfield traffic.

Yet the arrival and departure principles for both worlds are the same. Each airfield has a unique traffic pattern in the sky, known as a visual circuit. As long as all planes follow the same direction and heights within this circuit, whilst keeping themselves or being kept apart horizontally and vertically, all will be well. The common shape for a circuit is a rectangle, with the runway on one long (into wind) side and the downwind leg on the other long side.

Most circuits are flown to the left (i.e. you turn left after takeoff) but they can be to the right also, depending on the local topography or proximity of built-up areas. At most airfields you take off, climb straight ahead to 500 ft, turn 90° onto the crosswind leg, level at 1,000 ft and fly until you see the runway at 45° to one side, turn another 90° onto the downwind leg, fly parallel to the runway until it is 45° to one side, when it's time to turn 90° onto the base leg, descend and then make your last 90° turn to line up to land on the runway, known as the final approach. Some airfields are extremely busy training environments, with planes flying repetitive circuits, and with many planes in the circuit at once, so if you are inbound for landing, you'll always have to give way to any existing circuit traffic.

Thorough Planning Will Pay Off

The safest arrival at an airfield begins with good planning on the ground before your flight. You can research the location, size, shape and facilities of an airfield not only online, but also by referring to the airfield information handbooks or printed data sheets, which are usually updated annually. Visualize the layout of the airfield and note down all the key information in your flight log. With this to hand you will be all the more prepared to cope with arriving. Most busy airfields also continuously broadcast a recorded and frequently updated flight information service (AFIS) on a separate radio frequency, so make sure you listen to this! When you're about ten minutes away from the airfield, establish radio contact to find out which runway is in use and the pressure setting to dial

into the altimeter, so that when you land the altimeter reads zero.

You can prepare to join the circuit in one of two ways: usually you fly directly overhead the airfield, above the circuit traffic, and then descend and turn to follow the circuit; alternatively, you might be able to insert yourself into the circuit itself at circuit height on any of the three sides of the rectangular visual circuit, including flying directly to final approach. Whichever of the routes you take, stay alert and make sure you are following the checklist for your plane to prepare to land. In essence you'll need to slow the plane as you enter the circuit, and then prepare it to land (which includes security, i.e. making sure you and any passengers are strapped in) as you fly at circuit height along the downwind leg. Downwind checks include lowering the

Make smooth, gentle turns in the circuit. You'll be flying more slowly.

flaps and the undercarriage (if not already welded down). Remember, there are those pilots who have landed wheels-up by mistake, and all other pilots are waiting for it to happen! Once all downwind checks are complete, it's time – when clear to do so – to make the turn onto the base leg and start your controlled descent, ready to make your turn onto final approach. It's no wonder that circuits are a major element of the flying training syllabus. This is a demanding flying environment that rewards accuracy and finesse.

Sensations

Noise *Radio* There's often a lot going on around an airfield, and so the radio will be busy. Listen out if possible well before you announce you are inbound to land. You'll have picked up a lot of useful information already.

Feel *Controls* Don't confuse selecting controls such as the flap and, if appropriate, the undercarriage lever. You'll be busy, perhaps preoccupied, with maintaining your distance from other traffic, so make sure you positively select the right control by cross-checking with the relevant gauge or indicator lights.

Focus *Traffic separation* You need to know the whereabouts of any conflicting circuit traffic at all times.

A Useful Mnemonic Is FIRA

Use the airfield arrival mnemonic FIRA to ensure you are prepared for landing:
• *Fuel* Do you have sufficient fuel to make more than one circuit? If not, you have priority to land and need to declare this on the radio! Is the correct fuel tank selected if relevant?
• *Instruments* Is the direction indicator (DI) synchronized with the compass, and the runway landing heading noted or set on the DI?
• *Radio* Is the correct frequency set for the airfield (larger airfields may have more than one frequency).
• *Altimeter* Is this set with the airfield pressure?

Landing

Landing a plane is, like takeoff, a time for quick responses and vigilance as you will be flying slowly and close to the ground. No two landings are ever the same: some days you arrive with a delicacy and smoothness that make you smile as the wheels kiss the tarmac, but other days you feel as though the plane has a mind of its own.

Fly a Stable Approach

The key to a safe arrival is a stable approach, whether you are gliding, powered or flapless. Once you are established on the landing runway centreline, your goal is to fly an accurate, steadily descending flight path to your aiming point: the runway threshold, known as the numbers because the runway numbers are painted there. To achieve this, you must keep the perspective of the runway the same: if you're coming in too high, the runway looks noticeably long and narrow; if your approach is too low, the runway appears wide and short. Ideally the runway should appear larger and larger as you fly down the approach. Understanding this is pretty straightforward once you have flown, and mastering the technique comes with practice. Some airfields are equipped with approach indicator lights to help you fly down a stable path: red for 'too low', red–white for 'on glide slope', and white for 'too high'.

Once settled on the final approach, work diligently to fly and accurately maintain the correct airspeed, and be ready to make positive and rapid adjustments to the power to offset changing wind and atmospheric conditions. You may have set yourself up on a perfect approach path, only to find that the wind is flukey or changing force or direction without warning, known as windshear. If you're too high as a result, or overshooting, you'll need to descend rapidly: reduce power, lower the nose and increase drag by selecting more flap, if possible. If you're too low, you'll need to reduce the rate of descent, or fly level, or even climb if necessary to re-establish the best approach path: increase power and raise the nose.

As this demonstrates, more often than not you'll need to be making many corrections and adjustments to your flight path on the approach to land. This applies to all plane types, from a training plane to an Airbus. With practice this turns every landing into an enthralling challenge: to approach safely and to land smoothly where you intended, leaving you plenty of runway ahead to slow down without abusing the brakes.

Short Final…

The final moments before landing are known as 'short final'. This begins at about 200 ft (60 m) above the ground. At this point, when appropriate, select full flap and run through the essential pre-landing checks, which are particularly relevant if you are in command of a plane with a retractable undercarriage. Double-, even triple-check that the wheels are down. It is simply not sufficient to look at gear lights, or the position of the gear lever; you must prove to yourself that the wheels are down by cross-checking cockpit information, such as the position of the undercarriage lever (down) and the corresponding green light which indicates that the wheels are locked down. You cannot trust your senses from one observation, even if you're a highly experienced pilot with a disciplined attitude. This understanding is at the root of a well-known airline pilot joke that the co-pilot's only useful function in the cockpit is to double-check that the undercarriage is down and locked on final approach.

Keep the perspective of the runway constant as you descend on final approach.

As you round out, look forward and slightly to the left. This way you'll be able to judge how close you are to the ground.

Once you're about 20 ft (6 m) above the runway, it's time to prepare for the landing itself. You've arrived at your aiming point, so now transfer your attention to looking well ahead, and begin the roundout, or flare. Your goal is to touch down just as the plane is about to cease flying, when it will be controllable but at its lowest flying speed. Reduce power and pull back gradually to raise the nose and slow down your rate of descent. Look slightly to the left but forward to allow your peripheral vision to help you judge your proximity to the ground. Each type of plane has a different seating position and undercarriage layout, and

you'll find assessing depth a matter of practice, but with time the process becomes second nature.

When you're about a foot off the ground, check the throttle is completely closed and hold off by progressively pulling back on the control column. If you feel you're sinking too fast, ease back a little more; if you're climbing, known as ballooning, ease forward. Within a few seconds the main wheels will caress the ground (well, they ought to), but don't lower the nose wheel yet. You should keep the nose wheel off the ground until you feel that pulling back is no longer effective, and only then let it touch down. Track straight with the rudder, and if necessary use the brakes to slow down. Your landing is not over until you've left the runway. Stop beyond the holding point and complete the after landing checks.

Sensations

Noise *Engine* If you're making a glide approach, it will be unusually quiet with the engine at idle.

Feel *Controls* Make minor, smooth adjustments and keep the ball centred when turning. Keep a hand on the throttle throughout the approach so that you can power up or down without delay. *Vibration* You may be in for a surprise if landing on a grass strip: some are bumpier than they look from the air.

Focus Going around is not a sign of failure. Don't try to land when you are too low or too high, or if at any time you're not sure your approach is stable or accurate. Go round again: it's easier and safer.

Shutdown and Post-flight Checks

You may well feel that once you're on the ground your flight is over. In reality, as captain, you can only relax once you have parked, shut down, noted down any mechanical concerns and made everything secure. Taxiing and parking require vigilance and care, while the post-flight checks are a worthwhile discipline that will ensure the plane is ready and serviceable for the next flight.

Don't Get Complacent

Taxiing off the landing runway, you will not be clear of landing or takeoff traffic until you have passed the holding point or, if on a grass airfield, you are well clear of the active runway. Remember, planes that are landing and taking off have right of way and may also, like some taildraggers, have a restricted view on landing, so give plenty of room and be considerate to other airfield users at all times. Make a radio call to declare that you are clear, and if necessary to ask for directions to services or parking. As each airfield is different, this is not the time to be distracted as you fumble your way through your directory trying to make sense of an unfamiliar layout.

Once you are happy you are clear, and not obstructing the taxi area, stop and complete the after landing checks. If you are flying a plane with retractable undercarriage and flaps, make sure you double-check that the lever you are holding is indeed the flap lever. Every year someone, somewhere, raises the undercarriage on the ground by mistake, and it's not because of lack of experience. With your checks complete, it's now time to decide if you need fuel. Either a bowser, or fuel tanker, will come to you when parked or you'll need to taxi to the refuelling area.

Taxi at a walking pace, scanning from wingtip to wingtip, and also make sure that your taxi route will not blow up dust and debris at people, or the propwash damage any light planes or gliders. This is especially important when manoeuvring very slowly to park near a hangar or among parked planes, as you will need to increase power to complete tight turns and to make minor adjustments to your position. Try to park with the nose or tail wheel straight, which will make it so much easier to move off next time.

Leave Everything in Good Order

Once parked, apply the parking brake and let the engine run so as to allow the temperatures and pressures to stabilize within limits. Switch off the engine, and also the avionics and battery master switch. If you leave the battery master switch on you will flatten the battery, and this is bound to

happen just when you need the plane most urgently! Do follow your post-shutdown checklist, which will help to ensure you leave the plane ready for the next flight. Whilst you are in the cockpit, make a note of the flight time and also jot down any irregularities and minor technical issues that occurred during the flight. It's all too easy to forget these once you've left the plane. Better still, make a note of such snags as they occur. If the plane is rented, report defects of any kind to the operator. Make sure you remove all your belongings from the plane, and be particularly thorough as you do not want to leave any loose articles behind that may snag or obstruct the controls.

As you taxi to park, make sure you are well clear of other planes. Complete your shutdown checks methodically.

Secure the plane inside and out. This may involve securing or fitting locks to the controls, a cover to the pitot tube engine or air intake blanks, and locking pins as appropriate. If left outside, protect the plane with fitted weatherproof covers, which are not easy to handle on your own in a strong wind! Chock, or wedge, the wheels, and if there are tie-downs available, use them – so that the plane is ready for any weather. As you secure the plane, use your walk around to make any last checks of its condition and serviceability. Wipe off any oil or fluid traces from the fuselage or wings, which could be a sign of leakage, and again report these to the operator or, if this is your plane, remember to check for evidence again after the next flight. Finally complete any necessary paperwork for the plane, as well as for the airfield operator, and enter your flight times and observations in your personal log book.

Sensations

Noise *Engine* It's wonderful to sit back after shutdown, taking in the peace and quiet, and remembering the rewarding moments in your flight.

Feel *Controls* If it's gusty, hold the flying controls to prevent them flapping in the wind. *Brakes* Don't use the brakes against power: reduce power first.

Focus *Parking* Be extra vigilant when taxiing among parked planes. Look out at the wingtips to be sure you are clear and remember that you need plenty of space to swing the tail round.

Write down your flight times at shutdown and always make sure you have turned off all switches. Stop the controls from moving about in the wind by securing them with straps or pins.

3 First Flights

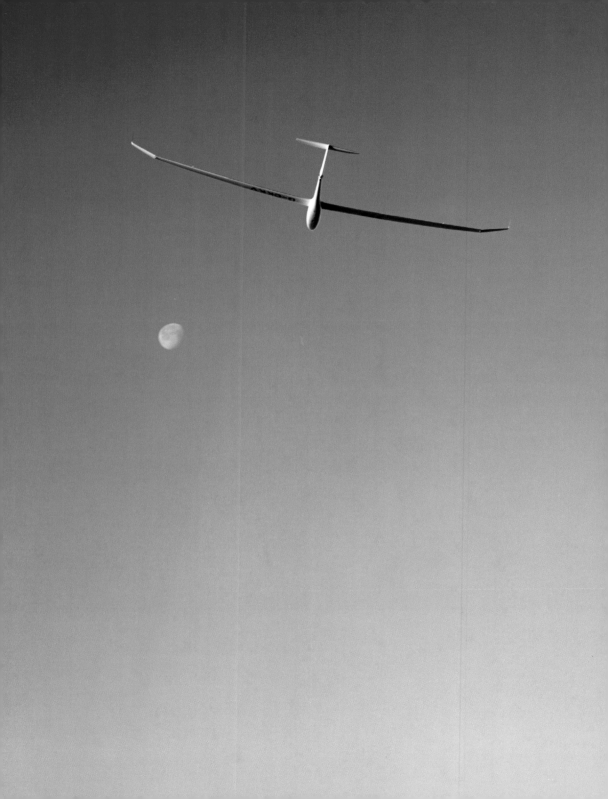

DG1000

High-performance Aerobatic Training Glider

Looking straight ahead, across the other side of the airfield, a steady white light glows on the cab of the winching machine. It's time to launch. A quick glance left along the slender 10-m (33 ft) wing to see whether your helper, holding the tip level, is ready; then a look to the right, to the launch chief who nods and swivels round to check the skies are clear before calling 'Take up slack' to the winch operator on his hand-held radio. The winch cable comes alive, slowly at first, and then snakes across the grass. The failsafe chain clinks as it tightens and strains against the weight of the glider, and you begin to ease forward. 'All out – all out – all out,' calls the chief, and the wheel beneath you starts bumping over the turf. An instant later you are airborne, pulled by the cable into the sky with a satisfying whoosh, followed immediately by the steady whistle of the slip stream: you're ascending in what seems like a near vertical climb at more than 3,000 ft (900 m) a minute.

Gliding is a pioneering aviation sport. There's nothing quite like flying without the complexity and noise of an engine. It's a truly satisfying experience that combines a unique selection of contrasting sensations – from bustling team work at the launch point to peaceful solitude in the air, from being hurled into the sky on a winch launch to the graceful, slow descent that follows, and from the exhilaration of soaring and cross-country flight to the trepidation of landing in a farmer's field when the lift from thermals disappears. And it's intensely addictive, providing inexpensive and rewarding flying within a thriving club environment, supported by a dynamic and coherent international fraternity.

High-performance gliders are designed for efficiency when soaring and have always possessed clean and often elegant lines. The traditional materials used to make gliders, wood and fabric, have latterly been giving way to composites (such as plastics reinforced with high-tech materials like carbon fibre), which have pushed performance to new levels. Leading this evolution for two-seater trainers is the DG1000, a glider that combines excellent soaring and cross-country performance with safe handling characteristics for all levels of training. Its curvaceous canopy is low-shouldered, providing increased visibility down and sideways, while its slender fuselage can be fitted with a fully retractable small engine and propeller to get you home if need be. The seemingly delicate T-tail houses an easy-access ballast compartment containing removable brass weights for optimizing the fore and aft balance of the glider, depending on the weight of the pilots, or solo pilot.

The DG1000 is also a particularly beautiful glider with a slender 20-m (66 ft) span including kinked wing extensions. Remove the extensions to transform it from

---

Wingspan 18 m (59 ft), or with extensions 20 m (66 ft)

Length 8.6 m (28 ft 1 in.)

Height 1.6 m (5 ft 4 in.)

Weight Empty 415 kg (915 lb), Max takeoff weight 750 kg (1,653 lb)

Seats 2

Speed Never exceed 146 kts (270 kph), thermalling 55–60 kts

Minimum sink rate in calm air 120 ft (37 m) per minute

Years of manufacture From 2002

Numbers produced 120 (mid 2007)

Cost New, from about £56,000– 76,000 ($109,000–147,000)

a competitive soaring mount into a fully aerobatic training glider. On the ground the DG1000 looks different too, with a perched stance that comes from an oversize main wheel mounted on a fully sprung oleo. This fully retractable, shock-absorbing main wheel is not just for comfort, but offers vital safety benefits in the event of a hard landing or landing on rough ground: the strong spring on the oleo is designed to help protect the pilot against back injury. In the cockpit there are other sensible features too: all controls, including undercarriage lever, are duplicated; and the seating positions are ideal, combining comfort, space and, crucially, a good view forward for the rear pilot (which is also the instructor's position).

Climbing into the front cockpit requires a certain relaxed dexterity that comes with practice: you end up sitting very low, with your legs supported yet raised, stretching out into the slender nose where your feet rest against the lightweight rudder pedals. As with all gliders, the instrument panel is small and, aside from the primary flight instruments, uncomplicated. Of great significance, however, are the particularly sensitive variometers – vertical speed gauges which show lift or sink – as well as a GPS. The cockpit is also uncluttered by levers and controls: the short and slender control column falls to hand, with the undercarriage and airbrake levers well positioned on the left-hand side.

There are two ways of launching a glider into the sky: either using a ground-based towing system, where a fine steel cable is attached to the glider and then wound onto a drum on an engine-driven winch (a winch launch); or towing it (an aerotow) on a fine rope behind a powered light plane, known as a tug.

A winch launch is dynamic and exciting, with swift acceleration and a fast climb. The glider also pretty much flies itself, bar the odd minor adjustment to keep the wings level, maintain best climb speed, or to combat any cross-wind. It's important, of course, to be prepared for winch failure or cable break, especially below 500 ft (150 m). Once the glider has been towed to the maximum height of the cable, the pilot pulls the cable release knob, and the cable – stabilized by a brightly coloured canvas drogue parachute – falls to the ground.

An aerotow is a very much more gentle affair than the winch, but one that requires precise flying as the glider is being pulled along behind the tug at about 65 knots (120 kph) with a 135 m (440 ft) synthetic fibre rope. The glider pilot's goal is to fly an attitude and position that ensure a maximum rate of climb and the minimum of stress to the tug. You can imagine how uncomfortable it is to pilot the tow plane if the glider, weighing more than 500 kg (1,100 lb), is being flown coarsely, erratically or out of line with either the direction or attitude of the tug. This is a time of dedicated technique and steady concentration combined with quick reactions, particularly near the ground. Once at the agreed tow height it's time to be set free, so look all around and especially in the direction you want to go, and with a pull on the cable release-knob bank sharply away from the tug, glancing out to confirm you are clear of each other as the tug heads for home. Roll out and ease forward on the control column to establish a best cruise speed of 60 knots (110 kph).

Savour the exquisite experience of being aloft without an engine. If your shoulders are tense and held high, now's the time to pull them down as you wiggle against the

harness, making a better contact with the character of this magnificent plane. Adjust your hearing to appreciate the whispering semi-silence and take full advantage of the magnificent view. For a 20-m wingspan, high-performance soaring machine, this is a sprightly, well-harmonized design that can be flown with fingertip precision. At the slightest indication of a thermal – the feeling of which varies from a gentle tremor to a violent convulsion of lift, confirmed by the variometer – you can turn steeply in an instant to start a circling pattern so as to remain within, and ride the energy of, the rising bubble of air.

You'll be able to turn tighter in a thermal at slower speeds, and here is where the DG1000 shows its design pedigree. Slow speed characteristics are entirely benign and predictable: there's no sudden drop of a wing, and the stall announces itself with a tremble, more like a sigh of exasperation for insensitive handling than a slap on the wrist. As with all gliders, you'll need good control coordination in the turns, matching the correct rudder input to the angle of bank for smooth, efficient flight. Simple, elegant aerobatics are effortless and supremely graceful as the slender wings provide a perfect reference for accurate loops and rolls, and the panoramic field of view makes for increased safety and enjoyment as you sweep from one manoeuvre to the next.

The DG1000 descends at about 150–200 ft (45–60 m) per minute at a 60-knot cruise speed. When, inevitably, it is time to land, this glider has very effective airbrakes that emerge from the top surface of the wing and are operated by pulling on an oversize, blue-coloured handle on the left-hand side, just below the canopy edge. Lowering the wheel is straightforward – a twist to release and a sharp pull on the undercarriage handle – and you're set to land. The way to land a glider accurately is to aim for a touchdown point just short of the threshold and then adjust your rate of sink with the powerful airbrakes. Sitting so low, it's easy to round out on landing a little too high, but it's not a problem if you do: hold the attitude, or ease forward a touch if you're very high, descend again, and when about a foot from the ground, reselect the landing attitude, and the glider will sink gently onto the main wheel as the wing finally loses lift. The well-sprung main wheel bumps and thumps across the grass without discomfort and you can lower a wing to the ground just before or as you come to a halt.

Silence. It leaves you trembling with excitement from the experience. This is a different sort of excitement from powered flight, more subtle and sensitive, more refined one might say. It's an experience that will linger with you.

Diamond Star DA40 TDI

Wingspan 11.9 m (39 ft 2 in.)

Length 8.1 m (26 ft 5 in.)

Height 2 m (6 ft 5 in.)

Weight Empty 795 kg (1,753 lb), Max takeoff weight 1,150 kg (2,535 lb)

Seats 4

Power 135 hp, Thielert Centurion 1.7 L Common Rail Turbo Diesel

Fuel Jet or Diesel, capacity 114 or 155 L (30 or 41 US gal), fuel burn @ 70% 18.5 L (4.9 US gal)/hr

Propeller 3 blade constant speed, 2 m (7 ft) diameter

Takeoff run 335 m (1,099 ft)

Rate of climb 650 ft (198 m)/min

Speed Never exceed 178 kts (330 kph), Cruise at 70% 125 kts (232 kph)

Landing run 287 m (942 ft)

Year of manufacture From 2000

Numbers produced Over 600 of all variants

Cost New DA40 TDI with glass cockpit, from about £185,000 ($360,000)

Exciting New Plane for Training and Touring

Training planes are not known for cutting-edge technology, and it is sad but true that most pilots have learnt to fly over the past forty years at the controls of inefficient planes with dull handling. No wonder so many newly qualified private pilots have found it hard to be motivated to expand their aviation horizons! Until recently, there were few obvious solutions, but you're about to be spoilt for choice with a variety of composite planes that are revolutionizing general aviation. One of the leading innovators is Diamond Aircraft Industries of Austria, which aims to combine the best use of materials, engine and navigation technology with safety, high performance and economy. An impossible challenge? The Diamond Star DA40 TDI is its answer.

Walking across the tarmac to the Diamond Star, it's a strange but welcome feeling to be excited by the shape and form of a single-engine training and touring plane. This plane has mirror-smooth, curvy lines, with a bulbous cockpit and elegant, slender wings, and it looks and feels efficient to the touch. Its design history is rooted in gliders – or, rather, motor gliders, where light weight, strength and maximum performance are second nature. The wings have not one but two carbon fibre spars, and it's no surprise that this plane has a higher safety factor rating than other metal planes in the same category. On each wing is a beautifully engineered fuel filler cap, from which the fuel is guided through a stainless-steel, scoop-like funnel to a tank that lies the length of the wing, sandwiched between the spars.

It's the type of fuel that makes this version of the Diamond Star so exciting and forward-thinking, however. By the cap are clear instructions to fill with jet fuel. This is a piston-engine-powered propeller plane with a difference. Lift off the tightly shrouded cowlings to look at the impressive engine. It's not a new design by any means, but a derivative of a Mercedes common rail diesel, which burns either jet or diesel fuel. This is an inline powerplant complete with a coolant system like a road vehicle. It's frugal, consuming 18.5 L (4.9 US gal) per hour in the cruise, quiet and supremely easy to control. In the cockpit, there's one lever instead of three for the engine and prop, so with one action this throttle lever controls the propeller, power and mixture – and there are no magnetos, and no carburettor heating control either. It's a straightforward, logical and intuitive set-up.

You'll find yourself idly stroking this beautifully finished plane. The laminar profile wings are narrow with flared winglets, and the fuselage tapers seemingly radically towards the tail. The one-piece canopy wraps around the cockpit and is all part of the upward-tilting hatch, affording a remarkable combination of ease of entry with maximum visibility. Back-seat passengers have their own door, complete with large side windows. The attention to detail continues within the cockpit. The seats are shaped and finished in the style of a quality motorcar, with plenty of space behind the passengers for light luggage.

Settle into the front and be prepared for another great leap forward. The panel comprises two flat screens. This is the Garmin G1000 Glass Panel Cockpit, and these two screens tell the pilot all he needs to know in a totally integrated package, from flight instrumentation to engine information, communications and navigation. Before long this will be interfaced with an autopilot to complete the ultimate user-friendly panel. As a back-up, there is a set of the three essential mechanical flight instruments and a standby compass above the screens. The control column is integrated into the front of the fixed seat, so it's out of the way of your legs but falls immediately to hand. The seats are fixed, but the rudder pedals adjust, which is a bonus for the rear passengers, and directly above, the canopy has been coated in a curving sweep of opaque white to provide protection from the sun.

The start procedure is as simple as a diesel car. Power on, and the screens come alive in a few moments. Then turn the key to Engine Start Master On position (so the glow plug warning is evident), wait for a few seconds until this message disappears, and turn the key again to start. With a brief growl the engine fires up and settles into a vibration-free whisper at idle. This liquid-cooled engine warms quickly and you're ready to taxi within minutes. Like a jet, once moving this plane taxis happily on a level tarmac surface at idle, and the exceptional view all around makes it easy to keep an eye out. There are none of the usual, rather complex, piston-engine checks. Merely press and hold the Engine Control Unit test button and then watch (and hear) the engine and propeller test themselves, with no input from the pilot whatsoever. This Digital Engine and Propeller Management system provides convenience and safety enhancements too, giving you more time to fly the plane.

Set flaps for takeoff, complete your checks and line up. Throttle up to full power, shown as a percentage on the screen, and leave it there. Acceleration is brisk, but wait until about 59 knots (109 kph) before easing off the ground. This is an efficient, low-drag wing, so let the plane accelerate to 70 knots (130 kph). By this time you'll be climbing at 650 ft (198 m)/min – above 400 ft (120 m) it's time to raise the flaps, producing some short-lived but evident sink. Within seconds of being airborne, you can sense the character of the plane – it's quiet, vibration-free, and possesses a remarkable field of view, even in the climb. The engine thrives at full power and feels completely unstressed, as well as turbine-like. Level off and the view over the nose is so good it feels as though you must be descending. Once level and at a cruise speed of 125 knots (232 kph), the power can be reduced to 70% (at this setting noise levels are even more subdued), and with full long range fuel you're good for nearly 1,100 nautical miles (2,000 km).

General handling is best described as refined and the plane feels really rigid, with excellent stability at all speeds, making this an ideal machine not only for cruising but also for instrument flight-training too. The primary flight display (in effect an oversize attitude indicator) makes it easy to scan flight information at a glance when manoeuvring

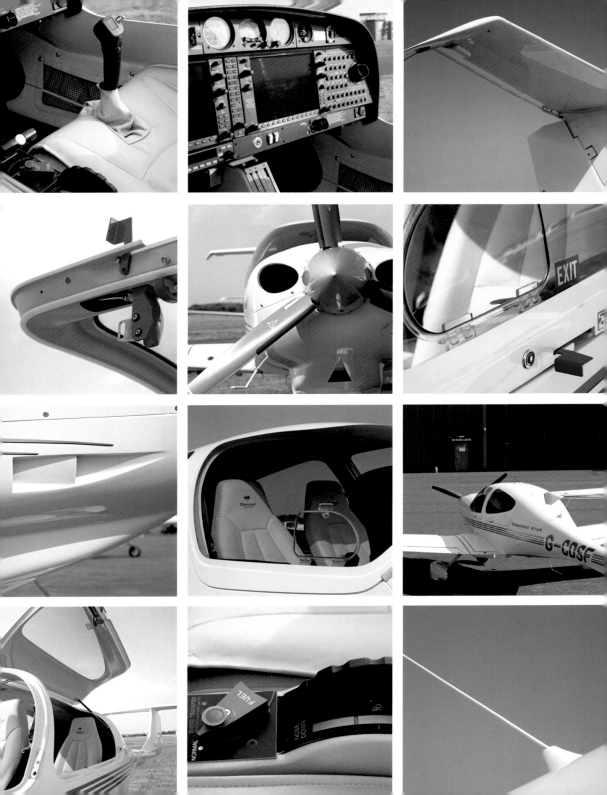

in good weather, and the modern slip indicator is exactly as found on an Airbus. Roll response is crisp and rewarding, and the good visibility makes it effortless to complete the frequent lookout checks. The wing is so efficient that the Diamond Star takes a while to slow down, and fully stalled will happily descend with wings level. You really have to pull hard to make it drop a wing and, when it does, it is a reluctant dip, easily corrected, rather than a rapid roll.

In flight, engine-handling is without fuss: the liquid coolant system ensures there's no risk of shock-cooling the engine during a glide, and the multi-function display makes accurate monitoring straightforward. As this sleek plane slows down reluctantly, descending in preparation for landing requires a little advance thought. Once set up on the approach, and with landing flaps selected, just nail 70 knots all the way down to the flare, close the throttle when the ground is but a few feet below you, and the plane will settle on the main wheels with smooth precision. If you come in to land too fast, the efficient wing will keep you flying – and floating along the runway.

As you might expect, shutdown is simple and quick, and with the canopy open you can just stand up and climb out, without having to stoop or clamber across the cockpit. When you walk away from the plane, look back. You'll be smiling, I assure you – not only at how pretty the plane is, but also at how much fun you've had. This is a plane for today, and about time, too.

Jungmann

Wingspan 7.4 m (24 ft 3 in.)

Length 6.7 m (22 ft)

Height 2.3 m (7 ft 5 in.)

Weight Empty 450 kg (992 lb), Max takeoff weight 720 kg (1,587 lb)

Seats 2

Power 150 hp, 4 cylinder Enma Tigre GIV inline

Fuel Avgas, capacity 90 L (24 US gal), aerobatic fuel burn: about 25–30 L (7–8 US gal)/hr

Propeller 2 blade fixed pitch, 2.3 m (7.5 ft) diameter

Takeoff run 150 m (492 ft)

Rate of climb 900 ft (275 m)/min

Roll rate 75°/sec

Speed Never exceed 162 kts (300 kph), Cruise 83 kts (155 kph)

Landing run 250 m (820 ft)

G limits +4 g, -2 g

Years of manufacture 1934–60 and limited CASA production 1989–90, limited production in Poland from 1990 onwards, and in Germany from 2007 onwards

Numbers produced c. 4,850

Cost Value now £40,000–60,000 ($78,000–117,000). New Polish: £71,000 ($137,000), German: £89,000 ($173,000)

Classic Biplane Trainer from 1930s Germany

Lying on your back in the shade of the wing, with a trickle of wind blowing across the grass, you revel in the warmth of an early summer's day. It was a terrific flight, the smooth air complementing the finesse and delicacy of the controls, as you looped, rolled and turned in a small pocket of clear-blue sky, and a perfect day for flying one of the world's most delightful classic planes, the legendary Bücker Jungmann.

There's not much shade under the lower wing, as the Jungmann is a petite biplane, but it's not stumpy or squat – quite the contrary, with its narrow, short wings, which are identical in size and completely interchangeable (each with ailerons), a short fuselage, and very simple, small horizontal and vertical stabilizers, onto which are suspended oversize elevators and rudder. The Jungmann was designed to be responsive. The tail sits low to the ground, or rather the nose is thrust up to the sky on a pair of splayed oleos. There's also a lot of pleasure to be found in the details of this design, and many advanced features too, considering its age – a lockable tail wheel, toe brakes and oil-damped sprung undercarriage, for example, or its strong fuselage (made of welded tubular steel) and all-wooden wings.

Designed by Anders Andersson, a Swedish aeronautical engineer, and Carl Bücker, a First World War German Navy pilot, the Jungmann first flew in the spring of 1934. The fusion of the Swedish and German design and engineering principles was highly successful, and their specification for this new biplane was a typically efficient one – to build a machine that was affordable, inexpensive to operate, robust and easy to maintain, and suitable for training new pilots as well as teaching aerobatics. From the first the Jungmann was a great success, and timely too, entering quantity production first for the German paramilitary force (Deutscher Luftverband or DLV) and by 1935 for the newly formed Luftwaffe, training their pilots throughout the war.

Most of the Jungmanns flying today, however, are ex-Spanish planes, known as CASA 1-131. Production of CASA Jungmanns continued until the early 1960s, with a further batch of ten made privately in 1989–90. From about half way through production, the CASA Jungmann was supplied with a Spanish-built Enma Tigre engine of either 125 or 150 hp, the latter almost twice the power of the original German 80 hp Hirth powerplant. Lift the starboard cowling and take a look at the simplicity of its inline four-cylinder engine – you can see at a glance how it works. You may as well wear the same grease-monkey overalls when flying too, as the engine can leak a little oil, but all these tribulations are completely in character with a classic biplane that responds to nurture and care. It's not just the Jungmann: there is a strong correlation between character in a light plane and its ability to drop or spray oil on your best trousers!

As you fasten the cowling, take a look again at the simplicity of its fasteners. There are only two on each side, and they are strong, effective, but light in weight and easy to use without the need for tools. And there are no bolts or levers on the four access panels to the cockpit: each is made of thin gauge aluminium that you can bend slightly, without fear of damage, to latch the lugs on the top corners of the panel into the fuselage frame. The magneto control – a gate with a removable sliding pin – is equally ingenious: when inserted, the pin makes electrical contact at each position; removed, the pin hangs on a chain and at a glance you can see the engine is safe, or rather that the prop is safe to handle.

You need to handle the prop every flight, both to prime the engine with fuel and to hand-swing to start. Chock the wheels (there's no parking brake) with the Jungmann facing into any wind, check the magneto pin is out and then pump twenty strokes on the wobble pump to generate some fuel pressure. The engine is primed with six to eight strokes of the plunger, swinging the prop six to eight times to suck the fuel into the engine. It's not hard to pull the prop, but it should always be treated as live, so as you swing move your hands and body down and away to the side. Now insert the magneto pin, make sure the mixture is rich and that the throttle is forward (cracked open) no more than half an inch and then swing the prop. The Tigre will start straight away.

Climbing into the back seat is not hard; you just need to be delicate and flexible. The cockpit is tight around the shoulders, but there's plenty of room within the fuselage, making you feel squashed, snug and comfortable at the same time! All the levers and controls fall to hand. The small windshield offers good protection from the slipstream, but it gets extremely cold in an open cockpit biplane, so dressing up warm and wearing a helmet with visor or goggles is essential.

Vigilance is required for all ground handling, especially when it's a windy day and the cross-wind picks up a wing: the opposite oleo compresses rather than tending to level the wings, so you need to make sure the wings remain horizontal with judicious use of the four ailerons. The free position of the tail wheel is ideal for manhandling the Jungmann – say in the hangar or a tight parking space – but at all other times it should be locked so that it is connected with the rudder pedals and steerable. You'll need to weave a lot when taxiing as you won't be able to see over the nose. The Jungmann may not be in its element on the ground, but it certainly keeps you on your toes, teaching an awareness and attitude you'll learn to appreciate.

Pre-takeoff checks are simple. If it's all clear, line up, making sure the wings are level to prevent any swing; if they're not, taxi forward to let the oleos settle equally before advancing the throttle. The Tigre is not a free-revving engine but lusty in its own way, and soon you'll be gently bouncing along, feeling the controls come to life. The rudder is very effective, making it easy to keep straight. Resist all temptation to raise the tail high: all this will do is compress the oleos, making the Jungmann lurch forward, and it will start to hop uncomfortably. Rather, raise the tail just a little, and let the Jungmann accelerate to about 45–50 knots (85–95 kph) and fly itself off the ground. Once airborne the springs on the undercarriage extend the oleos by between 23 and 30 cm (9–12 in.). It's a surprise to see the change of profile – and the Jungmann looks as though it is

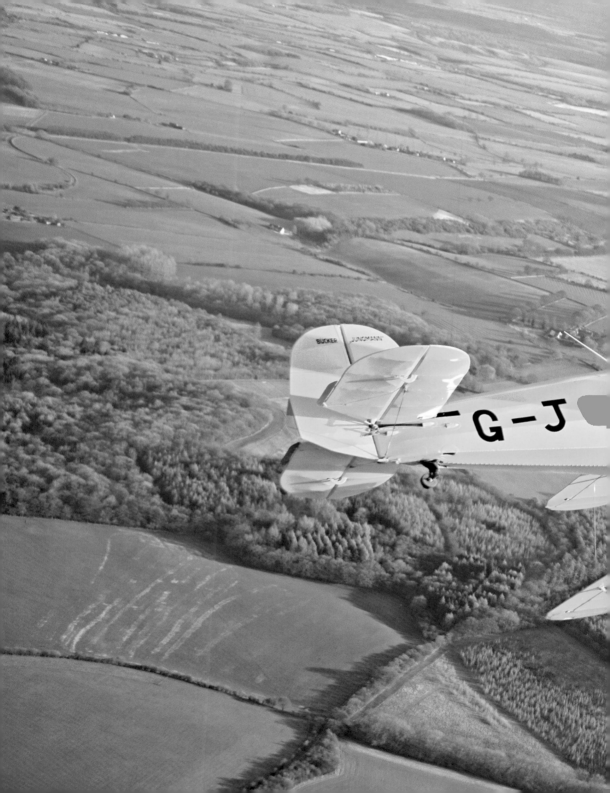

stretching forward when airborne – but this system ensures a soft arrival on landing. The Tigre settles at about 1800 rpm, so climb at 60 knots (110 kph). You'll be going up at about 900 ft (275 m) a minute, which is a lot better than most single-engine trainers of any age.

From the minute you leave the ground it becomes clear just what a special plane this is. The controls are sensitive and not twitchy, but what's truly extraordinary is the Jungmann's stability. Once trimmed in level flight, it will fly happily hands-off without deviation. Push forward or pull back, then release, and within a moment it settles back to level flight. In every way the handling feels natural, encouraging you to feel for the delicacy of pirouetting in tight turns and compact aerobatic manoeuvres. You'll feel so pleased with the tactile rewards of flying the Jungmann that you won't mind the array of wires and wings ahead of you, obscuring your view, and as you're turning and playing across the sky it's instinctive to look out for other traffic anyway. It's all about enjoying what's outside.

The magic speed band for aerobatics is between 90 and 110 knots (165–205 kph): from here you can pull into a tight little loop, aileron roll sweetly, climb vertically and pivot around a stall turn in an instant, and slow roll with such control that the nose feels pinned to a single point on the horizon. The fixed pitch propeller keeps you alert: the Jungmann accelerates surprisingly quickly in a dive, so you'll need to throttle back to prevent the engine overspeeding, and then go to full throttle again as you pull up. Stall and spin characteristics are also entirely straightforward: the CASA

Jungmann stalls reluctantly at about 40 knots (75 kph) and spins with a textbook entry and recovery.

Snap rolling? This is the forte of the Jungmann, well served by its large rudder and elevator, so that a snap roll or multiple snap rolls are smooth and predictable, without any jerkiness or hesitation. Start at about 65–70 knots (120–130 kph) by pulling back on the stick, make a slight pause and then apply full left rudder as quickly as you can. As the plane spins round, ease forward on the stick to maintain the rate of roll, and when you want to stop, release the rudder pressure. You stop, instantly. But you don't want to stop – you want to turn and roll, you want to loop and swoop. It's a magical sensation.

You won't have any problems landing, especially on grass and into wind. In the descent, set about 1200 rpm; as you slow, you'll need to trim all the way back. If you let go of the stick the plane flies all the way down the approach, settling at about 55 knots (100 kph) – just the right speed and attitude to arrive over the threshold, ready for you to close the throttle and be eased onto the ground on all three points. Even at 40 knots there's plenty of control authority and, once on the ground, you can track straight with the steerable tail wheel. It's best not to touch the brakes unless you have to, and until you are going very slowly you should only press on the toe brakes when the rudder is straight.

Once the engine is silent, sit still for a moment and look around you. You've just flown one of the world's most magnificent flying machines – in many ways, the first sport plane in a modern sense. Even now, no one makes a plane that comes close to the Jungmann for teaching both the important qualities of airmanship and the sweet pleasures of flying, with a true sense of freedom and grace. The Jungmann is a timeless work of aeronautical finesse and a joy to fly.

Sukhoi 29

Unlimited Aerobatic Trainer from Russia

You don't need to stand up close to appreciate that this is one of the most remarkable light aircraft ever made. The wing is thick, almost blunt-edged, and totally symmetrical, the fuselage is short and dominated by a jet-fighter-like bubble canopy, and one glance at the massive size of all the control surfaces raises the pulse. Derived from the single-seater Sukhoi 26, which dominates unlimited aerobatic competitions on the world stage, this machine is an ultra-dynamic, agile performer.

Closer inspection reveals a construction quality and materials specification that would not look out of place on a supersonic interceptor. And, indeed, this plane was designed in the early 1990s to a no-expense-spared specification by a team of the world's most imaginative aerospace engineers in Moscow. Sukhoi is a name associated with exotic, high-performance military aircraft, and the pedigree is clear – from its forged titanium legs to its full-length, extra-wide ailerons. Stainless steel, Kevlar, carbon fibre, titanium and Nomex honeycomb – the stuff of space ships – have all been used to make this aircraft light and immensely strong.

Swinging open the one-piece canopy, it's obvious that the design philosophy extended to the pilot's needs too. The pilot in command sits in the back, which affords an excellent view in the air but next to zero forward visibility when taxiing, taking off and landing. Between your legs and to the sides, clear vision panels provide an extra viewing dimension. The carbon fibre seats are raked back to give more g-tolerance, the forged magnesium rudder pedals support your whole foot and are intricately designed to be light but strong, and with a long travel (ideal for aerobatics). Getting in, you have to negotiate your way around what seems like an unnecessarily oversize control column, which is tall as well as thick but strangely frictionless and delicate. Sitting against your parachute, the seven-point harness snaps together and is tightened with two large ratchets that pin you to the plane – a necessary discomfort since this machine flies pretty much any way up. Up front are a big prop and a round engine, which, once you're used to the idiosyncrasies of this tough and powerful nine-cylinder Russian radial, is a reliable and ideal powerplant for the stresses and strains of rolling and tumbling flight. There are two simple rules, however: never wear new clothes near one (result: oil spattering or worse) and always check for any oil sitting in the lower cylinders (result: broken engine) before starting, which is a noisy event invariably accompanied by a swirl of blue smoke. These engines rumble and throb when relaxed and roar when worked hard, so that in a good aerobatic display you'll enjoy watching a truly sensory spectacle.

As soon as you start taxiing, you realize you have very little forward visibility, so make sure you weave left and right continuously to clear your forward view as much

Wingspan 8.2 m (27 ft)

Length 7.3 m (24 ft)

Height 2.9 m (9 ft 6 in.)

Weight Empty 788 kg (1,737 lb), Max takeoff weight 1,217 kg (2,683 lb)

Seats 2

Power 365 hp, 9 cylinder M14P supercharged radial

Fuel Avgas, capacity 260 L (69 US gal), aerobatic fuel burn: at least 100 L (26 US gal)/hr

Propeller 3 blade constant speed, 2.5 m (8 ft 4 in.) diameter

Takeoff run 150 m (492 ft)

Rate of climb 3,150 ft (960 m)/min

Roll rate 360°/sec

Speed Never exceed 243 kts (450 kph), Cruise 146 kts (270 kph)

Landing run 350 m (1,148 ft)

G limits Solo, aerobatic (55 L/14.5 US gal) fuel only: +11 g, -9 g

Years of manufacture 1993–2003

Numbers produced 69

Cost New £96,000 ($185,000), Value 2007: £125,000–145,000 ($241,000–280,000)

as possible. This is not a complicated plane and there are very few checks before takeoff: on lining up, lock the tail wheel straight, hold steady with the toe brakes as you ease the big throttle handle forward to 70% power, make a last-minute check of the engine instruments, and then let go of the brakes and increase the power steadily to the maximum. At first it's all a fast-moving blur, such is the acceleration and the overwhelming bellow from the supercharged radial. You can't raise the tail to see forward as the propeller would hit the ground, but within seconds the Sukhoi leaps into the air without needing any control input and climbs away lustily, at over 3,000 ft (900 m) a minute. It takes less than two minutes for you to climb 1 mile (1.6 km) into the sky. You're ready to play. This is not a plane to dawdle about in, and such is the climb rate and energetic performance, you'd be unlikely to practise for longer than twenty minutes at a time. Yet, when preparing for aerobatics – making clearing turns and climbing for height – the 29 feels delightfully sensitive and wholly manageable.

Let's have some fun. Monitor the engine controls and instruments, set the power to the maximum continuous setting and then forget about it. Tighten straps and check for loose articles: roll upside down and hold it there – you're likely to see or feel anything that falls – before rolling upright again. Pull back and roll left, sweeping skywards, looking outside all the while. There are few distractions on the instrument panel, other than essential engine and flight instruments. You'll soon realize that this plane likes to be flown with verve, to be manoeuvred, and after a while feels uneasy unless rolling, turning, looping and, with more practice, tumbling and snapping too.

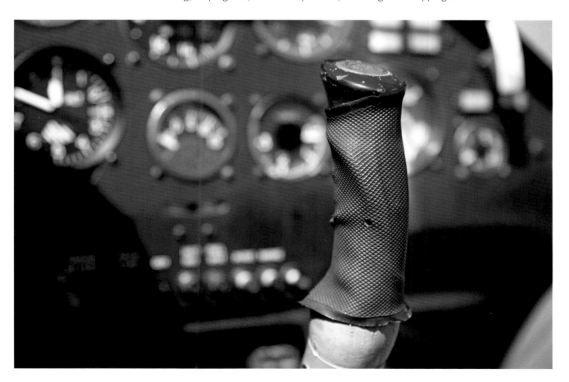

Want to roll? Pitch up a little, push the stick hard over to the left or right, and in less than one second you'll have rolled round the horizon – whap. Starting the roll is easy; stopping precisely takes practice. You'll appreciate the massive control column as it's reassuring to hang on to! When you really want full and totally positive inputs, take it in both hands. This works well for the climbing vertical roll. Pull back, just so at first, and then harder. The nose rears up. Once beyond about 70° on your way to the vertical, look out to the wingtip-mounted sighting pole, first left then right, as you guide the tips to sit equally on the horizon, with the sighting pole perfectly vertical. Pause – there's time – and then roll. By keeping both hands on the column grip, you can accelerate the sweep of the column to one side, and also make sure there's no pull or push in the action so you stay vertical, and round the Sukhoi goes in one full turn....

Loops, barrel rolls, snap rolls, lomcevaks (vertical tumble), ruades (tumble on a 45° upline which soon becomes a tumble earthwards)...these and so many more aerobatic figures to develop and practise, and so much control to play with, to explore. This plane feels so capable, so rewarding to experiment new moves, and yet it pays to be disciplined before fatigue sets in. You've no idea how drained you are until you shut down after an intensive flight, and later still when you wonder where strange bruises and aches originated. Physical fitness helps. This plane also respects practice. For full performance, you need skill, sensitivity and, crucially, understanding. It took the best Russian aerobatic pilots years to master the full potential of this remarkable and gratifying plane – so take your time, and enjoy the ride.

P-51D Mustang

Legendary American Warbird

It's an unmistakable sound, a deep, powerful growl mixed with a drawn-out pleasing whistle, and then a smooth whoosh as the Mustang flattens out of a dive and angles in a swooping turn along the crowd line, showing its distinctive pointy nose, curvy canopy and squared-off wings. Pulling up with a graceful, flowing roll, the sun cascades off the polished aluminium panels as the Mustang turns and prepares for another low-level flypast.

There were three very special allied fighters of the Second World War, and of these the Spitfire and the Mustang were powered by the same design of engine, the illustrious Rolls Royce Merlin. The third fighter, the Russian Yak 9, is less well known. All three types are flown today, and no air show would be complete without the presence of one or more of these very special planes. They have also long held top bill in most, if not every, pilot's wish list of planes they dream of flying. The world-renowned centre for Mustang training and operations is Stallion 51, based at Kissimmee Gateway Airport, Florida. Stallion 51 operate not one, but two of the rare dual-control P-51D Mustangs, the TF-51, both emblazoned with their name: 'Crazy Horse'.

It's no coincidence that this plane was named after the tough and graceful feral horse of the American West. These are the very characteristics that made it a successful fighting machine. Designed by North American aircraft to an urgent British requirement for a new fighter in April 1940, the first prototype flew 178 days later, in October 1940 – an extraordinarily short gestation period. It's not a petite fighter, like the Yak 9, or graceful like the Spitfire, but the Mustang looks practical, tough and ruthlessly efficient, and two pioneering design features were crucial to its success. Close up, the Mustang is a big machine, with an almost oversize slab-shaped wing – but look across the profile and you see a streamlined laminar flow design. Result: same drag as smaller wings on other fighters of the era, but more capacity inside the wing for lots of fuel, guns, ammunition, as well as a sturdy undercarriage. Secondly you'll notice just how aerodynamically clean this plane looks, complete with its futuristic oval intake forward of the extended pot belly of the plane, where the oil and engine coolant radiators are housed. Air enters the intake, flows over the radiators, is warmed and vents to the rear, creating some jet thrust. The result: very effective engine cooling with residual thrust which balances the drag from the intake almost exactly. In essence it's a zero-drag design – ingenious!

This is a plane you have to climb up into and it's immediately apparent that its cockpit design was well ahead of its time. There's space to move and store charts, adjustable rudder pedals with toe brakes, a height-adjustable seat, a simple lock for flight controls and tail wheel, and an instrument panel and control layout that has been designed for ease of use. Trim controls fall to hand on the lower left-hand side,

Wingspan 11.3 m (37 ft ½ in.)

Length 10 m (32 ft 9½ in.)

Height 4.2 m (13 ft 8 in.)

Weight Empty 3,232 kg (7,125 lb), Max takeoff weight 5,488 kg

Seats 1 (TF-51 dual-control version with 2 seats)

Power 1,695 hp Packard Merlin V-12

Fuel Avgas, usable 681 L (180 US gal), cruise fuel burn 246 L (65 US gal)/hr

Propeller 4 blade constant speed, 3.4 m (11 ft 2 in.) diameter

Takeoff run c. 335 m (1,100 ft)

Rate of climb 5,000 ft (1,500 m)/ min at full military power

Roll rate 90°/sec

Speed Maximum speed 380 kts (700 kph)

Landing run c. 275 m (900 ft)

G limits +8 g, -4 g

Years of manufacture 1940–45

Numbers produced 15,875

Numbers airworthy Approximately 150

Value now c. £720,000 ($1.4 m) for P51-D and c. £1.1 m ($2.1 m) for TF-51

the fist-sized throttle is comfortable to grip, and the engine and flight instruments are straightforward. Undercarriage and flap levers are robust-looking, down on the left-hand side, but far enough apart and in a contrasting shape and direction of movement to make inadvertent selection pretty unlikely. Engine cooling is automatic, with simple switches for manual override, and by the base of the control column the fuel tank selector is a model of effective design. Surprisingly the control column is slender and topped with an almost delicate grip. Most remarkable of all, however, is the seating position. This is a fighter you ride on, not one you're encased within – there's no sense of claustrophobia and you can't help swivelling round to appreciate the panoramic view.

Starting the Merlin is the usual five-handed affair, as you juggle with starter, ignition and primer switches and mixture control. There's a gentle sway as the propeller turns and then, with a barely perceptible lick of flame from the exhaust, the Merlin comes to life with a deep rumble. It's not a jiggling vibration, but a pleasing, soothing and massaging rumble, with the occasional pop and bang too. The elevated position allows pretty good forward visibility for a tail-wheel plane, but you still need to weave to clear the view ahead of the long nose when taxiing. With the control column held back the tail wheel can be turned 6° left or right with the rudder pedals.

On reaching the runway holding point, look behind to make sure you won't blow over a light aircraft and then, with the control column held fully aft, power up to 2300 rpm. Now you begin to feel the tremendous power of the Merlin as the Mustang trembles against the brakes and the torque of the propeller pushes the left wing down against the oleo. This is a helpful reminder to dial up 6° of right rudder trim to help counteract the swing to the left as you power up on takeoff. When you're ready to take off, open up the power steadily – not slowly, but steadily – all the way to 55 inches on the manifold pressure gauge, and keep the control column back as the plane accelerates. It's exciting: there's the thrill of the noise, the gloriously smooth delivery of power and the blur of acceleration. Maintain the back pressure until the plane accelerates to 50 knots (95 kph) and then slowly – and, yes, this time slowly – ease forward and let the tail rise. You're letting the tail rise rather than pushing the nose forward; this way the tail is ready to fly and the rudder will be fully effective against the torque.

At 90–95 knots (165–175 kph) the plane's ready to fly. Ease back a touch and you become airborne and accelerate fast. The landing gear limiting speed is 150 knots (280 kph), so raise the nose, check the engine temperatures and pressures at a glance, and raise the undercarriage. This is a simple and quick process, and once clean the Mustang continues to accelerate effortlessly and climb with gusto. To preserve the engine, it's best to power back to 42 inches and 2500 rpm when at a safe climb-out height. As soon as you move the throttle, you need to compensate for the change in torque with rudder, and then trim out the rudder pressure. Within minutes, rudder-trimming as you change speeds becomes pretty much intuitive and you realize just how comfortable and pilot-friendly the Mustang is, rewarding sensitivity and understanding.

Level out, and the speed builds quickly. Again, retrim then set 37 inches and 2300 rpm. You're now cruising at a true air speed of about 270 knots (500 kph). The nose-low attitude of the Mustang at cruise is unsettling at first, as the view over the nose

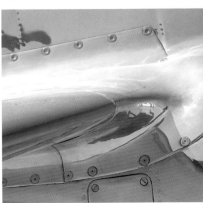

is so good it feels like you're descending. Get used to it. And then rack the Mustang round in a turn and enjoy the resolute steadiness of this forgiving fighter – pull harder and, instead of flicking or departing, there's a rumble and a tremble asking you to ease off.

There's no drama in the stall either, and the Mustang recovers flying composure merely by lowering the nose. Loop – no problem! A steady pull from the cruise and let the energy work with you as you soar skywards, guiding the nose back to earth again with judicious use of the rudder to maintain the display line. Same again for the barrel roll. Take your time – it's best to let this plane flow, there's so much energy and impetus in hand that you can transition smoothly from simple manoeuvre to manoeuvre.

This machine is elegant but also slippery and takes time to slow down when you have to prepare to land. Again, as the power and speed decrease, you wind off the rudder trim, and then enjoy the stability of the design. The flaps are effective, and the excellent view over the nose makes it straightforward to fix a stable approach speed of 110 knots (205 kph), coming back to 100 knots (185 kph) over the threshold before rounding out at 90 knots and letting the wide-track undercarriage smoothly bear the weight of the Mustang. You wheel it on, slightly tail-down, at about 80 knots (150 kph), and then lower the tail gently.

Park the Mustang alongside a Spitfire and marvel at the contrast in design and scale, and yet together they share the same historic engine. The Spitfire looks like a handmade, delicate interceptor, curvaceous and lady-like, and not easy to manufacture or maintain. The Mustang is a complete contrast: solid with lots of straight lines, machined rather than crafted, logical in design and effective in action, straightforward to build and easy to maintain – this was the first truly modern, multi-role combat plane.

Hawk

Renowned British Military Jet

There's something thrilling about strapping into a Hawk. From the front seat, there's nothing in front of you – no propeller, no engine bay or cowlings, no canopy struts. Everything moulds and curves towards a slender nose. You're also not sitting next to anyone, and it's a snug fit, which makes it feel like this really is your cockpit. But it is what you're sitting on that really sets it apart – the rocket-powered ejection seat, which does wonders to sharpen the mind!

Once you're in the jet, time literally flies by in a blur of action and focused concentration, in complete contrast to the lengthy, methodical and painstaking preparation beforehand. In the UK, the Royal Air Force and Royal Navy use the Hawk for jet conversion and advanced weapons training, so each flight – known as a sortie – is varied in profile, from low-level navigation to slow flight, stalls and spinning. Your clothing, equipment and training have to cope with not only these extremes, but also the seasons. From late autumn to late spring the sea temperature around the UK cools to between 3 and 8°C (37–46°F). At this time of year pilots need to don an all-in-one protective immersion suit to keep out the fast-numbing cold in case of an ejection over the ocean, not to mention countless other layers and equipment including a g-suit (to help prevent blackout and g-induced loss of consciousness), life jacket (LSJ) and ejection-seat leg restraints – around 20 kg (44 lb) of clothing all in all.

Walking to the jet, you glance along the perfectly arranged lines of black Hawks being readied by the ground crew and engineers for another busy day training future RAF combat pilots. The Hawk first flew in August 1974, and it's a tribute to the design team that even now – more than thirty years on – it still looks modern, effective, sleek and exciting. Waiting by the steps, the ground crew are ready to help you make the last preparations before flight. Climb carefully up to the edge of the cockpit, and before you get in make sure the ejection seat is safe by checking that the small, bright-red T-handled pin is in place just under the ejection handle.

Once seated, start the sequence of connecting yourself umbilically to the aircraft. There are two connectors from the LSJ to the left-hand side of the ejection seat: the first is attached to the personal survival pack (PSP) in the seat, containing your one-man dinghy; the second, the personal equipment connector (PEC), is a combined g-suit, oxygen and radio/intercom supply plate, which snaps into place in an instant. Thread the restraining cords through the leg restraint eyes across the front of the shins and click them into place on the seat. In the event of an ejection these cords tighten, pulling your lower legs tight to the seat. Place the quick release fitting (QRF) against your midriff and then secure the left and right lap straps, followed by the shoulder straps.

Wingspan 9.4 m (30 ft 10 in.)

Wing area 16.7 sq. m (179.6 sq. ft)

Length 11.9 m (38 ft 11 in.)

Height 4.0 m (13 ft 2 in.)

Weight Max takeoff weight 5,700 kg (12,566 lb)

Seats 2

Power Rolls-Royce / Turbomeca Adour 151 non-afterburning turbofan with 5,200 lb thrust

Fuel Avtur, capacity 2,804 lb (1,272 kg), max range with internal fuel c. 1,000 nm (1,852 km)

Takeoff run 589 m (1,800 ft) at max takeoff weight

Landing run 488 m (1,600 ft) at normal landing weight

Time to height Takeoff to: FL (flight level) 100 in 1.6 mins, FL 200 in 3.8 mins, FL 330 in 7.6 mins

Roll rate 135°/sec at sea level

Speed Maximum speed 572 kts (1,059 kph)/Mach 1.2

G-limits +7.2 to -3 g, never exceed +8 g and -4 g

Years of manufacture 1974–present

Numbers produced 900 (early 2007)

Cost now Undisclosed

You need to dial into the ejection seat your weight in kilograms, including your extra equipment. This minutely adjusts the angle of the rocket pack under your seat to ensure exactly the right trajectory if an ejection were necessary. The ground crew hands over your helmet, which also contains your headphones. The microphone is within the oxygen mask, dangling from the side of the helmet. Connect the oxygen mask to the supply pipe, and your radio/intercom lead to the socket on the side of the LSJ, and lower the helmet's clear visor, which should be kept down throughout the sortie.

It's time to close the canopy. You'll notice that it's patterned with lines: this is the miniature detonating cord (MDC) designed to shatter the canopy a split second before you eject, and, like the seat, it is made safe on the ground with a red T-handled pin. Arm the seat and the MDC by removing their respective pins and stow them in their holder, which indicates to the ground crew that you're ready to go. From the back seat the view forward is excellent, affording the instructor a truly commanding position. A pair of short, curved mirrors give you a panoramic view to the rear three quarters, which is important when you're watching your tail. There's a reinforced glass screen separating the two cockpits so that, in the event of any damage to the front windscreen, the instructor is protected and can take control. Notice too how lean and functional the cockpit is, from the oversize but short throttle handle to the large flight instruments, and by contrast the selection of small switches and dials for engine, hydraulics and electrics. There are no levers at all for undercarriage or flaps, which are controlled with small push buttons and switches. Rising sturdily from the floor and falling immediately to hand is the control column, its handgrip topped by the knurled elevator trim switch and a variety of gun, bomb and camera controls.

On start-up you'll hear a rumble, followed by a gentle hiss. Release the parking brake and ease forward on the power to roll forward, bringing power back to idle once on the move. For steering, touch the differential brakes on the tips of the rudder pedals to control the deflection of the nose wheel. Unlike a piston-powered plane, there's no warm-up period to speak of. You start up, taxi, line up on the runway, and pause…as you hold the Hawk with the toe brakes, slide the throttle to full power. The engine takes about seven seconds to spool up with a muted roar. Feel the nose wheel compress and the nose dip as you reach 95% power, then 100%.

Ready? Release both brakes and you spring forward, pressed into the seat and accelerating smartly, yet with a smooth and glorious push in a straight line. Up to 50 knots (95 kph) steer with full rudder and dabs of brake, and thereafter the rudder becomes fully effective, so drop the heels to the floor and concentrate on using the rudder for directional control. At 90 knots (165 kph) it's time to raise to nose. This is a positive aft movement of the stick, and an equally steady pressure to hold the nose off as the Hawk accelerates to 120 knots (220 kph). It's time to fly!

Rotate the nose skywards and you're away. Within seconds you can raise the landing gear and mid flaps. Soaring skywards at over 5,000 ft (1,500 m) a minute, the controls feel light, sensitive and yet positive. At first you might find yourself chasing an attitude, so that the Hawk weaves and oscillates a little, but you just need to relax your grip. This plane is intuitive to control, so let it fly with you.

Once level, you'll soon find how sensitive it is in pitch – ease back a touch and you'll be climbing at 1,500 ft (450 m) a minute. Want to roll? Keep your feet still and deflect the control column to the side, and the Hawk rolls in an instant, smooth and fast, yet precise to control, returning smoothly and accurately to wings level. More aerobatics? You'll need 4,500 ft (1,370 m) above you to complete a loop at 300–350 knots (555–650 kph). Slide the power forward to the stop, ease back, keep the wings level as you're pressed hard into the seat and feel the g-suit grip in a steady 4.5 g pull up. When over the top, ease off the back pressure a fraction and keep the wings level on the horizon. As you accelerate rapidly earthwards, bring the power back to 90% and pull to level out where you began.

Stalling is usually practised above 10,000 ft (3,000 m) for a safe recovery margin (stalls should be recovered by 7,000 ft/2,100 m). At the practice height, and with clearing turns complete, bring the power all the way back to idle, maintain straight and level with back pressure, and at 200 knots (370 kph) lower the gear and mid-flap to simulate the landing pattern. You'll be able to fly the Hawk all the way down to less than 115 knots (210 kph) in this configuration, and although there's some mild buffet and a tendency to roll, this is easy to correct with the ailerons. Select full flap and, once in the stall at 105 knots (195 kph), you're in complete control – initially descending at 500 ft (150 m) and then 1,000 ft (300 m) a minute, and soon increasing, nose up, to more than 6,000 ft (1,800 m) per minute. To recover, ease forward and apply full power: in an instant you're flying again and you quickly climb back to a safe altitude.

Up for some spinning? No problem, but you need more height for the spin and recovery: 28,000 ft (8,500 m) is a good height, and you need to be at least 15,000 ft (4,600 m) above cloud. Maintaining a good lookout, select idle

and start a level medium turn, letting the speed bleed off to about 165 knots (305 kph). Double-check the throttle is closed and then simultaneously and smoothly pull the control column back to the centre and apply full rudder in the direction of the turn. Hold and maintain these inputs: the Hawk rears up and rolls into the turn, although not alarmingly, and pretty quickly establishes a spin, rumbling and buffeting all the while. The speed stabilizes initially at about 150 knots (280 kph), but you're plummeting pretty fast – at over 15,000 ft a minute. By the fourth turn you're edging towards 180 knots (335 kph) and it's time to recover from the spin. Centralize rudder and control column and in an instant you're in a dive.

You'll be smiling with the exhilaration of the dive, but going so fast uses up a lot of height, so it's time to ease back to level flight. Bring the throttle all the way back to idle and slide back the toggle switch on top of the throttle lever to deploy the airbrake. The deceleration is abrupt and you're thrown forward, although not unpleasantly. There's very little pitch change, and the speed unwinds from about 550 knots to 300 knots (1,020–555 kph) in what feels like a few seconds. This is a slippery plane and so the airbrake is essential for moderating speed quickly – particularly when joining a formation and approaching to land. Approaching another Hawk from loose to close formation (7–9 ft/2–3 m apart) demands faith in the use of the airbrake: as you streak towards your leader with a 50 knots overtake speed, within 150–225 ft (45–70 m) select airbrake, ease back on the power, watch the closing rate unwind and then fly up alongside and slot into place whilst jockeying the power forward and closing the airbrake.

Most low-level training in the UK takes place within dedicated low-flying areas (LFA) in sparsely populated countryside which are pre-booked with assigned time slots for the military. LFAs are not exclusive zones, and so it's crucial to keep a good lookout. At a steady 420 knots (780 kph), you're enjoying a sensational ride at 7 miles (11 km) a minute, and minor turbulence results in a soft cobblestone ride and tremor. Woods, fields, and hills flash by. As a town or village approaches, avoid overflying with a quick jink to the side. Here comes a turning point, so turn, NOW, and pull to 4 g, with your g-suit gripping hard. At 4 g you're four times heavier, and it soon becomes hard, sweaty work…here's the new heading, NOW, so roll level again and speed on.

By the time you've been airborne for about 55 minutes, you're not only approaching a return-to-base (RTB) fuel state, but also beginning to tire. There's only so much you can take before performance and learning deteriorate in a fast jet. 'Echelon left, GO' calls the leader. Power up and turn towards him, closing from slightly below and wide, and then ease up and in, so that you're tight alongside. Your leader guides the formation to fly down the centreline of the active runway in the direction of landing, and one by one you break to the side into the circuit, following the leader's flight path with sufficient spacing to make an oval circuit and land one at a time in quick succession.

You're the last to break, so stay level and straight and count to 'three bananas'. On three, make three simultaneous inputs. Roll and pull hard, close the throttle and deploy the airbrake. Crank the Hawk round, in a 5 to 6 g turn, accurately following the leader's flight path, and watch the speed come back. Roll out. At 200 knots select the airbrake in, punch the gear down, select mid flap, and trim.

You are now running downwind, parallel to the landing runway. Pre-landing checks complete, start to power up the engine to 78–80%. By the end of the downwind leg you're flying at 150 knots or so. Start your final turn and guide the nose positively down, and select full flap and trim again as the Hawk pitches nose up, so that the speed reduces to 130 knots (240 kph). The runway threshold speed you need is easy to calculate: add one knot per 100 kg (220 lb) of fuel remaining to 110 knots. Ahead of you in the distance the leader should have cleared to one side of the runway, so you're good to land.

Aim for a steady and stable approach. It's easy to master in the Hawk. Ease back a little and, approaching the threshold, let the speed decrease. As the ground comes up at you, there's a rush of speed sensation, but no matter – look well ahead and, as you cross the numbers, check your speed, close the power and ease back just a touch. The undercarriage jolts and shudders as it soaks up the energy of your arrival, and the nose goes down pretty much simultaneously. Now decelerate and keep straight by pressing on the toe brakes. Soon you're at walking pace, so clear the runway and complete the after landing checks, including replacing the seat and MDC pins before returning to the line. Shutdown is simple and quick, and as the canopy opens the fresh air feels really good.

This may be a military trainer by design, but the Hawk has all the pedigree, performance and equipment of a compact fighter jet. Its excellent performance, allied with its simple systems, makes this jet an ideal instructor's plane too. In the Hawk you'll spend more time learning and refining your flying skills rather than dealing with systems. This is a genuine, honest and fun jet to fly – the perfect machine for making and moulding the best pilots.

Learjet 45XR

Luxury Jet with an Iconic Pedigree

Built more than forty years ago, the Learjet has become synonymous with rapid and luxurious air travel for privileged corporate executives and the wealthy. From the very start, its super-sexy, rakish design oozed speed and appealed to dynamic individuals with a lack of patience – two legendary characteristics of Bill Lear, the American founder of Learjet.

Lear was sixty-one years old when he took up the challenge to produce one of the world's first business jets. The majority of his competitors were all established aircraft manufacturers designing small jet transports for the military or government use. It was the early 1960s, a time when business travel was provided by slow, unpressurized, propeller-driven planes, and yet passenger jets were crossing continents at high speed in the smooth air above any bad weather. Lear was determined not only to get up there, but also to climb faster and cruise higher than any airliner.

Such was the energy and drive of Lear and his team that they were able to fly the first Learjet Model 23 on 7 October 1963, confounding all critics who believed that only an established aerospace corporation could produce such an advanced and sophisticated jet plane. Several features of the original Learjet were truly revolutionary and exciting and remain evident in production models to this day, including the instantly recognizable T-tail, the super-streamlined, panoramic two-piece windshield and, to a lesser extent, the clamshell main door.

Today Learjet is part of Bombardier, the world's third largest manufacturer of civil aircraft, and continues to produce fabulous-looking and successful business jets, one of which is the Learjet 45XR. At first sight this nine-seater – or eight-seater if you discount the aft lavatory, which has a seat belt and is certified for occupancy during takeoff and landing – is undoubtedly a Learjet, with its compact, purposefully pointed shape and profile, classic windscreen and T-tail, but in many ways the resemblance ends there. The Learjet 45XR (and also the six/seven-seater Learjet 40XR) is the first entirely new-design Learjet since the first Model 23. Yes, some of the original and now iconic features have been retained, but more than £250 m ($500 m) was spent to create a new generation Learjet that possesses not only superlative performance, benign handling characteristics, ease of operation and maintenance, but also meets commercial airliner design and safety certification standards in both the USA and Europe.

Walking to the Learjet 45XR makes you appreciate its exquisite lines. First of all, it is low-slung, with a long and slender fuselage that tapers into an elegant, sharp nose. The wings and curved wingtips (winglets) are beautifully clean, and the T-tail rakes back as if moulded by the force of the high-speed airflow. Polished aluminium

Wingspan 14.6 m (47 ft 9 in.)

Wing area 29 sq. m (311.6 sq. ft)

Length 17.6 m (57 ft 7 in.)

Height 4.3 m (14 ft 2 in.)

Cabin width 1.6 m (5 ft 1 in.)

Weight Max takeoff weight 9,752 kg (21,500 lb)

Seats Up to 9 passengers and a minimum of 2 crew

Power 2 x Honeywell TFE731-20BR turbofans of 3,500 lb thrust each

Fuel Maximum fuel weight 2,750 kg (6,062 lb), maximum range with 4 passengers and 2 crew 2,087 nm (3,865 km)

Takeoff run At max takeoff weight at sea level, at 15°C (59°F), 5,040 ft (1,536 m)

Speed Maximum speed Mach .81 (465 kts/860 kph)

Landing run Less than 811 m (2,661 ft) at sea level, depending on landing weight

Numbers produced 314 Learjet 45 and 45XR models manufactured (January 2007)

Cost now c. £5.8 m ($11.5 m)

is used sparingly but beautifully for efficiency as well as detailing, emphasizing the oversize cabin windows, the shape of the windshield, the sweep of the wing, winglets and horizontal stabilizer as well as the perfect circle of the engine intakes. Close up, the quality of the finish and the level of attention to detail are simply fabulous – it will make you want to run your fingers idly along the wings and the nose!

You don't climb up into a Learjet 45XR, but step into it. The unique clamshell door also doubles up as access steps and an entrance canopy, and once closed is secured with twelve pins, as the door is part of the fuselage structure. The cabin is well lit by the sixteen windows, and more roomy than the slender fuselage suggests. You won't be able to walk down the central aisle unless you are less than 5 ft (1.5 m) tall, but it's not uncomfortable at all to move about the cabin.

This may be a fast business jet, built to fly on instruments, but there's no excuse not to enjoy the view. The two-pilot cockpit is dominated by the wrap-around windshield. The cockpit is compact – it has been said that getting into the pilots' seats is 95% of your conversion training on the Learjet 45XR! It's not hard, however, and there's an overhead grab-handle that allows you to hold off your weight as you ease yourself into the ample and adjustable seat. You're perfectly positioned in the pilot's seat to admire the array of screens across the glass cockpit.

There are four large colour screens: two are the primary flight displays (PFD); the third is a multi-function display (MFD), showing navigation, weather radar and traffic avoidance system (TCAS) information; the fourth (EICAS) displays engine information and the crew alerting system, which provides the crew with a warning checklist in the event of any necessary action. Two further small screens sit below the three standby flight instruments, providing visual representation of radio, navigation and identification data. If the main screens become unusable, these two small screens can also show navigation and engine data. All of these screens can present data either schematically or digitally.

Throughout the cockpit, the switches and controls are laid out in a logical fashion, clustered according to system. The cockpit environment is dark: if none of the buttons is lit up, then all's well. In common with most passenger jets, the autopilot controls are just below eye level on the coming, and this is where most of the flying is controlled. The floor-mounted control column is topped with a yoke, complete with transmit and pitch trim buttons.

Start-up is simple. With power levers in the idle detent, reach down on the central pedestal and press one start button. Monitor engine indications, and then start the second engine. There's a subdued whine of power well behind you, and after a few further checks you're ready to taxi. Once rolling, leave the power at idle; steer with the rudder pedals, and brake as necessary with the toe brakes. Line up for departure, advance the power levers to the takeoff detent, and within eight seconds the engines have wound up power and you're surging along at an effortless and relentless pace. The sensation of smooth acceleration and speed is terrific. Steer as necessary with dabs of toe brake. Depending on the weight, temperature, wind and elevation, you'll raise the nose at somewhere between 110 and 117 knots (204–217 kph): with a positive back pressure,

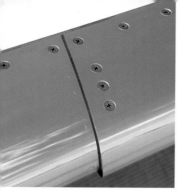

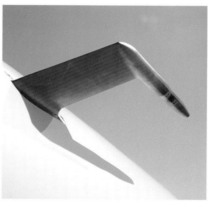

ease the nose up, initially to between 15 and 18°; with the undercarriage and flaps up, let the nose sit steady at about a 12–14° climb attitude; soon you'll be at the best climb speed of 250 knots (465 kph), zooming skywards in legendary Learjet fashion.

At around 5,000 ft (1,500 m), at a speed of 250 knots, disengage autopilot and make some level turns. The technique for smooth tracking around the horizon is to roll, set the bank angle, and then immediately ease back on the yoke. You'll need to be positive about keeping the back pressure constant and steady. At 250 knots you can fly with one hand only; above this speed, it's harder work and you'll be more comfortable and effective with both hands guiding the yoke. Full control deflection will give a roll rate of about 80°/second. Rolling out? Be ready to simultaneously trim and ease forward to prevent any vertical acceleration. The visibility all around is excellent, but there are no cues in the cockpit to set against the horizon and fly the turns visually – so in good visibility you'll be glancing in at the attitude indicator and out again to maintain an accurate, level turn. This is a plane that revels in being flown precisely.

In the stall this Learjet is totally predictable, due to the stabilizing force of the aft-mounted delta fins. Slowing down is not easy in a Learjet 45XR, and once the flaps and gear are down, at idle power, you'll need both hands to continue to ease back on the yoke to maintain level flight. At 119 knots (220 kph) or so, you'll have the nose some 12° up, but keep hauling back on the trembling yoke, right the way to full aft position; at 105 knots (194 kph), and just as the stall bites, your ears are deafened by the shout of 'STALL, STALL' in your headset. Try to survive this repeated warning whilst flying in the stall, completely in control, keeping the wings level with aileron inputs only. It's hard work holding back against the delta fins' forward-pitching action, and in a fully developed stall you descend at about 3,000 ft (900 m) a minute. To recover, relax the back pressure and apply max continuous power. Once at a safe flying speed of about 130 knots (240 kph) and accelerating, ease back slowly and climb again at 250 knots.

The Learjet 45XR is a remarkably docile, high-performance T-tail jet at slow speed, and it's therefore no surprise that the approach and landing are straightforward. The field of view is excellent for joining an airfield circuit, and with flaps and gear down you can hold about 114 knots (211 kph) in a steady descent with 60% power. As you near the threshold, a quick look at the radar altimeter confirms you are at 50 ft (15 m), so retard the power levers to idle and maintain a nose-up attitude of 3° – letting the Learjet 45XR sink. There's an audio countdown: begin to ease back to flare and let the trailing-link landing gear ease you comfortably onto the runway. Allow the nose to touch down gently and brake as required. Once clear of the active runway, it makes sense to taxi on one engine. Shutdown is simple too: pull up the power lever and ease back to the shut-off position.

Parked up, when all's quiet, sit back for a moment and savour your fortunate position. You're at the controls of a truly modern Learjet 45XR which, like the original model, flies and performs like a fighter, and with effortless ease at all speeds – exactly as Bill Lear intended.

Airbus A380

Superjumbo of the Future

You've really no idea just how big the A380 is until you stand under the rear of the aircraft. The tail towers above you, reaching over 24 m (79 ft) into the air, but most extraordinary is the size of the horizontal stabilizer. Its surface area is about the same as the wings of the small twin-engine Airbus A320 series, which carry between 100 and 185 passengers, and looking forward, you're presented with a forest of undercarriage wheels, twenty-two in total. This is the world's heaviest passenger plane, weighing in at around 560 tonnes (1,235,000 lb) when fully loaded, some 225 tonnes more than the early versions of the Boeing 747 jumbo jet, and it needs this many wheels to distribute its weight so as not to damage any existing airport surfaces. Step back and admire the wonderfully complex, yet elegant trailing-edge profile of the wing: it's slender and totally smooth along not only its length but also in profile; there are no partitioned sections, like all other airliner wings to date, and its four engines are exactly in proportion with the scale of the machine. It's also more swept back than any other Airbus, ensuring that this is the fastest of the family, but you will get an idea of just how versatile it is across the speed range, such is the size and spread of the flaps that extend down and along the massive streamlined flap guides. The A380 is also, quite remarkably, as slow on the approach to land as the diminutive A320 series.

The cockpit is more like a room than a compartment at the sharp end of a plane, and there's plenty of space for two or three extra pilots' seats. The windows are deep and wide, and not raked back too dramatically, and their scale and profile are in keeping with the sense of being in a well-lit room. Your seat looks oversize and there is a large void between the seat and the rudder pedals. All Airbus planes designed after the A300 series are controlled by a diminutive side stick controller, positioned to hand on the left- and right-hand cockpit walls. There's no control column or yoke on the floor, and you can't help but smile as you take in the extra space. Each seat is electrically controlled with push buttons, and, when at its full aft position, motors to the side away from the central pedestal, allowing you to squeeze through the gap and sit down. It may look odd at first, and it feels even more odd sitting in the seat with no floor-mounted control column, but after taking a few seconds to adjust the rudder pedal height and distance, your left hand (the left-hand seat is where the Captain sits) grasps the side stick controller instinctively.

Considering how wide the cockpit is, and the fact that this is the world's largest airliner, there's a surprising lack of systems panels and switches. This is down to the successful development of a unique man machine interface (MMI) philosophy throughout the Airbus family, where electronic controls (including fly-by-wire),

Wingspan 79.8 m (261 ft 8 in.)

Wing area 846 sq. m (9,104 sq. ft)

Length 73 m (239 ft 3 in.)

Height 24.1 m (79 ft 7 in.)

Fuselage diameter (horizontal) 7.1 m (23 ft 5 in.)

Weight Max takeoff weight 560 tonnes (1,235,000 lb)

Seats Up to 853 passengers and a minimum of 18 crew

Power 4 x Rolls-Royce Trent or 4 x GP 7200 turbofans of c. 70,000 lb thrust each

Fuel Avtur, capacity 310,000 L (81,900 US gal), range with typical passenger load: 8,000 nm (14,820 km)

Takeoff run At max takeoff weight at sea level, at 15°C (59°F), 2,990 m (9,810 ft)

Speed Maximum speed Mach .89 (589 kts/1,090 kph), cruise speed Mach .85 (562 kts/1,041 kph)

Landing run From between 1,600–2,100 m (5,250–6,890 ft) at sea level depending on landing weight

Years of manufacture 2006—present

Numbers produced 166 on order (early 2007)

Cost now c. £175 m ($338 m)

automation and semi-automation have been incorporated into the entire design. Moreover, Airbus has always sought familiarity for flight crews throughout the range, with the same cockpit layout and operating procedures, which makes training a whole lot easier. Like other Airbus and the more modern planes, you're seated in front of an array of liquid crystal displays – in this instance, eight in total, with a single set of standby analogue flight instruments. Autopilot controls are to hand on the face of the coming on top of the panel, and overhead are the engine, hydraulics and fuel control switches. If a problem occurs, a warning light flashes either amber or red in front of the pilot (depending on the severity of the emergency), the emergency drills are presented electronically on one of the screens, and the relevant controls are illuminated. The central pedestal houses the throttle levers, spoiler and flap levers, the T-handled parking brake lever and the communications and navigation control units.

The glass cockpit is taken to a new level of sophistication in the A380. The screens are extra tall, so that more information can be presented. The two primary flight displays show the flap and spoiler configuration and the pitch trim setting, in addition to the speed, direction, altitude and attitude. There are two displays for navigation (essentially large GPS screens), an engine/warning display and a systems display, which can show data in either a pictorial form (for instance, the wing of the aircraft with fuel tanks and volumes within each tank) or in a tabular form. This systems display is sandwiched by two new design multi-function displays (MFDs), which are controlled by a track ball in combination with a qwerty keyboard and provide an interface with the flight management system, so you can, for instance, enter data for departure and arrival which then links seamlessly with the navigation screen. You can also show normal checklists on the systems display screen, which are smart as well as interactive. An action message is displayed in blue and turns white when the correct reaction is taken. For the ultimate in paperless cockpits, pull out your onboard information system – a full-size qwerty keyboard and touchpad, complete with screen (behind the side stick).

Surrounded by such electronic sophistication, it's no wonder the start-up is simple. There are four flat-topped toggle switches: you move a pair forward on each side to start two engines at once, monitor the temperatures and pressures, and you're done. Taxiing is also straightforward: you can steer and brake with the rudder pedals on the straight taxiways and use the direct action rudder tiller to the left of the side stick for tight turns. There is also a video camera (the external and taxiing camera system or ETACS) mounted high up on the leading edge of the tail fin which clearly indicates the position of the rear section of the fuselage and the wheels underneath.

The engines are computer-controlled to deliver just the right amount of power for your needs, so as to reduce wear and tear. Advancing the thrust levers, there's a very subdued roar and instant acceleration, which is smooth and steady, taking you rapidly to a typical rotate speed of between 140 and 160 knots (260–295 kph), depending on takeoff weight. With a small movement of the wrist you've eased back to a climb attitude of about 12° in order to maintain the initial climb speed of about 250 knots (465 kph). Call to the co-pilot for gear up and then start to retract the flap as you climb away at over 2,000 ft (600 m) a minute. For some pilots, the hands-on flying stops here, as

airline procedures may dictate engaging the autopilot at 1,000 ft (300 m) above the ground, and indeed the A380 has been designed for autopilot operations, complete with autothrust, speed control and, of course, autoland.

When ready to level out, ease the nose down. You instinctively reach for the trim wheel, but there isn't one! It's all automatic. There is a manual back-up control on the central pedestal. Now select a handling speed of 250 knots and move the thrust levers back to the CL (climb) detent on the quadrant. Autothrust automatically engages. To turn to the left, all you have to do is to gently move the side stick to the left and then let go. The A380 deploys a combination of up to three ailerons and six spoilers (of a total of eight) per wing and so banks to your input, and then continues the turn with majestic serenity and precise, predictable control. Rudder input? No need: the roll and yaw coupling is fully automatic. This is terrific for the passengers, guaranteeing a particularly smooth ride at all times. Any turns up to 33° of bank will be flown precisely according to your input, but when you bank harder (to a maximum of 67°) and then let go, the A380 is programmed to roll back and stabilize at 33° of bank (and in pitch you cannot raise the nose higher than 30° or lower than 15°). All the while this huge plane responds and flies like a small plane – it's very rewarding to fly and surprisingly agile.

For slow speed flight, cancel the autothrust and speed control, and close the thrust levers to idle, whilst maintaining height. Deploy the spoilers to slow down more rapidly and then lower gear and full flap and spoilers – known as Config Full. As you approach the stall, you've applied full aft stick with the nose raised to about 14° and

you're flying at only about 118 knots (219 kph). Now lower the nose and power up, and let's go home.

Set autothrust and speed control – we'll hand-fly the approach to land. Downwind, select flaps and spoilers to the first setting (known as Config 1): your speed stabilizes at around 180 knots (335 kph). Make a wide, sweeping smooth turn onto final and select Config 2. Once level, call for gear down (this takes about 20 seconds from moving the lever to locked down), and then Config 3 and within a minute Config Full. You're now flying with about 2.5° nose up, at around 135 knots (250 kph), down the centreline and on the glidepath. The precision approach lights on either side of the threshold are your external reference. At 50 ft (15 m) a computer-controlled voice calls your height, so it's time to begin a slow flare, easing back on the side stick to about 4.5° nose up. At 20 ft (6 m) another warning call is issued, immediately followed by the sharp command 'RETARD – RETARD', which you shouldn't take as a comment on your flying skills! Bringing back the thrust levers and holding the pitch attitude steady, the A380 settles smoothly, leaving you to lower the nose gear to the tarmac. The sixteen spoilers deploy on touchdown in automatic mode. Once you've lowered the nose wheel, select reverse thrust, which is fitted on the two inboard engines only. Start braking gently below 100 knots (185 kph). You'll need to slow to a taxi speed of about 8 knots (15 kph). If you need some help finding your terminal stand, select zoom on the onboard airport navigation system and you'll find a detailed airport map depicting the aircraft's exact position. This facility is particularly useful for identifying runways – many large airports have multiple as well as sets of parallel runways too.

What a plane. It's a machine full of extremes and contrasts. Small handles control big movements with delicacy and precision. Computers, seemingly complex and overwhelming at first, provide truly useful information. It's fast in the cruise, and slow to land, yet it's efficient too, consuming when fully loaded about the same amount of energy per passenger mile as a family car. Controlling the world's largest passenger jet with fingertip finesse makes for a truly memorable experience.

Pilot's Notes

There's no single source of useful information for aviators, such is the varied scope and complexity of the interrelated worlds of aviation. However, the notes that follow will guide you to all the relevant sources of further information as well as goods and services – whether you want to buy a trial flight as a gift or are looking for a career as a pilot.

Specific Interests

Gliding
UK: The British Gliding Association provides all the information you need about gliding, and also publishes *Sailplane & Gliding Magazine*. Go to www.gliding.co.uk.
USA: Soaring Society of America: www.ssa.org
Australia: www.gfa.org.au
European Gliding Union:
www.egu-info.org
France: www.ffvv.org
Germany: www.segelflug.de
New Zealand: www.gliding.co.nz
South Africa: www.sssa.org.za

Microlights
UK: The British Microlight Aircraft Association is the recognized body for this sport and their periodical is the *Microlight Flying Magazine*. Go to www.bmaa.org.
USA: www.airsports.fai.org (microlights and ultralights)
Belgium: www.fed-ulm.be
Canada: www.upac.ca
Denmark: www.dulfu.dk
(Danish ultralight association)
Europe: www.europe-airsports.fai.org
          www.ulmeurope.com
Germany: www.daec.de
          www.dulv.de
          (trikes and para motoring)
Ireland: www.irishmicrolights.ie
Italy: www.ulm.it/default_en.htm
Malta: www.islandmicrolightclub.com
Spain: www.sportec.com/fae

Aerobatics
UK: The British Aerobatics Association runs glider and powered aircraft aerobatic competitions. Go to www.aerobatics.org.uk, and for international aerobatic competitions see www.iac.org.
USA: www.american-aerobatics.com
Australia: www.aerobaticsaustralia.com.au
Brazil: www.acrobrasil.com.br
Canada: www.aerobaticscanada.org
Finland: www.taitolento.fi
France: www.france-voltige.org
Germany: www.german-aerobatics.de
Italy: www.aeroweb.lucia.it/en/sports/
Scandinavia: www.skff.nu
South Africa: www.aerobatics.co.za
Switzerland: www.saa.ch

Military Aviation
UK: The Ministry of Defence website, www.mod.uk, provides links to the RAF, Fleet Air Arm and Army Air Corps.

Flight Safety
UK: GASCo is a charity which works to improve flight safety in all forms of general aviation.
Go to www.gasco.org.uk.
USA: Air Safety Foundation: www.aopa.org/asf/

Accidents
UK: The UK Air Accidents Investigation Branch (AAIB) is part of the Department for Transport and is responsible for the investigation of civil aircraft accidents and serious incidents within the UK. Go to www.aaib.gov.uk.
USA: www.ntsb.gov/aviation/aviation.htm
For worldwide accident investigation branches, go to: www.gasco.org.uk/pages/page.asp?i_ToolbarID=3&i_PageID=116

General Information

AOPA

The Aircraft Owners and Pilots Association represents the interests of aircraft owners and pilots, and is part of a worldwide forum. See also their periodical, *GA Magazine*.
UK: www.aopa.co.uk
USA: www.aopa.org
International: www.iaopa.org

Royal Aero Club

This is the national coordinating body for Air Sport in the United Kingdom. Go to www.royalaeroclub.org.
USA: www.eaa.org

CAA

The Civil Aviation Authority is the UK's specialist aviation regulator. Go to www.caa.co.uk.
USA: www.faa.gov

PFA

The Popular Flying Association promotes the safe and economical operation of recreational aircraft and publishes the magazine *Popular Flying* (www.pfa.org.uk).
USA: www.eaa.org
European air sports: www.europe-airsports.fai.org

General Aviation Magazines

Widely available, these magazines and their excellent websites make it easy to find a flying school near you.

UK

Pilot: www.pilotweb.co.uk
Go Flying: www.pilotweb.co.uk
Flyer: www.flyer.co.uk
Today's Pilot: www.todayspilot.co.uk
Loop: www.loop.aero

USA

Flyer: www.flyingmag.com
Plane & Pilot: www.planeandpilotmag.com
Air & Space: www.airspacemag.com

Australia/New Zealand

Australian Flying: www.yaffa.com.au
Flightpath: www.yaffa.com.au
New Zealand Aviation News: www.aviationnews.co.nz

South Africa

SA Flyer: www.saflyermag.co.za
African Pilot: www.africanpilot.co.za

Pilot Supplies

UK

Transair: www.transair.co.uk
Pooleys: www.pooleys.com
The Flying Shop: www.adamsdirect.co.uk
AFE: www.afeonline.com

USA

Aircraft Spruce: www.aircraft-spruce.com
Sporty's pilot shop: www.sportys.com
Pilot shop: www.pilotshop.com

For a list of European pilot shops:
www.flyingineurope.be/pilot_shops.htm

Cooperators

Airbus: www.airbus.com
Bombardier: www.bombardier.com
Diamond: www.diamondair.com
RAF: www.raf.mod.uk
Shell Aviation: www.shell.com/aviation
Stallion 51: www.stallion51.com

www.howtoflyaplane.co.uk

For lots more photos, links and a diary of displays with or by Nick Barnard.

People

From start to finish this has been a fun project – and made possible by the generosity and commitment of the providers or owners of the planes we flew.

DG1000
Helen Evans, Peter Masson, Gordon MacDonald, demo pilot Ed Lockhart and the Lasham Gliding Club

Diamond Star DA40 TDI
Bob Green and demo pilot Henrik Burkal, Malcolm Gault at Cambridge City Airport

Jungmann
Peter Scandrett

Sukhoi 29
Gene and Patrick Willson

P-51D Mustang
Lee Lauderback, demo pilot Eric Huppert, camera plane pilot John Posson, Angela and Kelly, all at Stallion 51

Hawk
AVM Chris Harper, AVM John Ponsonby, Air Cdr Brian Newby, Gp Capt Tony Barnby, Wg Cdr Chris Huckstep, Wg Cdr Richard Jacobs, Sqn Ldr Jim Schofield, Sqn Ldr Mark Byrne, Sqn Ldr Ros Hyde, Flt Lt Karen Needham, Flt Lt Craig Needham, 19 Sqn pilots: Capt (USAF) Drew Dougherty and Flt Lt Greg Sagar as well as 208 Sqn pilots: Flt Lt Chris Lyndon and Flt Lt Jamie Norris. Keith Dennison and Russ Eatwell.

Learjet 45XR
Alec McRitchie, Murray Sutherland, Marc Miller, Bethanie Unruh, Brenton Saunders and demo pilots Marty Unrein and Chris Barnett, Kerry Swanson and Rick Rowe

Airbus A380
Barbara Kracht and Elisabeth Ahlbäck, Tore Prang, Frank and Elisa Chapman

Illustrations
Peter Bull created all the illustrations, flawlessly

Thanks also to:

Peter Scandrett, Colin Hutson, David Eno and Chris Huckstep, who helped bring sense and clarity to the first and second sections. Other helpful comments were provided by Richard Goode (Sukhoi), Reinhard Rötzer (Jungmann).

Lucy for making visual the spirit of this book

Camilla for understanding so much

Paul Beaver, Rob Midgley, Jeremy Diack and Willy and Debs Hackett, for ideas and sharing contacts

Jez for being so generous